D1605284

In Memory of

Jim Ellis

2017

Fly Fishing and Fly Making For Trout, Bass and Salmon

by J. Harrington Keene

with an introduction by Roger Chambers

Self Reliance Books

Get more historic titles on animal and stock breeding, gardening and old fashioned skills by visiting us at:

http://selfreliancebooks.blogspot.com/

Introduction

I am pleased to present yet another title on Fishing and Fly-tying.

This volume is entitled "Fly Fishing and Fly Making" and was published in 1898.

The work is in the Public Domain and is re-printed here in accordance with Federal Laws.

As with all reprinted books of this age that are intended to perfectly reproduce the original edition, considerable pains and effort had to be undertaken to correct fading and sometimes outright damage to existing proofs of this title. At times, this task is quite monumental, requiring an almost total "rebuilding" of some pages from digital proofs of multiple copies. Despite this, imperfections still sometimes exist in the final proof and may detract from the visual appearance of the text.

I hope you enjoy reading this book as much as I enjoyed making it available to readers again.

Roger Chambers

Made by C.F. ORVIS, Manchester, Vt
COPYRIGHTED.

Made by C.F.ORVIS. Manchester.Vt

PREFACE TO SECOND EDITION.

In the following pages I have endeavored to give in a plain, precise and practical manner the essence of what I have learned of fly-fishing and fly-making in two continents during the past twenty-five years. I have not concerned myself with literary elaboration and finish. The design was to be *useful*, and the information given has therefore been mercilessly boiled down to a solid extract.

There seemed a need for such a work, especially in connection with the subject of American fly-making. The capture of the first salmon, trout or bass on a fly of the angler's own manufacture is the beginning of a new era to him. He tastes an entirely new sensation with a zest hitherto unknown. Many works describing fly-making in the land of Walton exist, but no practical fly-tier has hitherto attempted to specifically instruct the *American* fly-fisherman. This work is intended to fill the vacant niche in the piscatorial library.

I have reason to know from the many correspondents who have written me, that the first edition was appreciated, and as this present issue contains almost double as many pages, fully illustrated, it is not unreasonable to expect that its usefulness will be found greatly enhanced, and commensurately valued by the great army of my brother fly-fishermen.

JOHN HARRINGTON KEENE.

GREENWICH, WASHINGTON CO., N. Y.
  January 1, 1891.

CONTENTS.

FLY-FISHING AND FLY-MAKING.

CHAPTER I.

THE SENSES OF FISHES IN RELATION TO THE FLY-FISHERMAN.

In order to arrive at a right method in the capture of any of the *fera naturæ* it is unmistakably necessary to first become acquainted with the creature's personal habits. No man in his senses would go out to trap—say, beaver— knowing nothing of the tastes, faculties and general intelligence of the animal, nor would the ordinarily sensible man expect to get much sport with his gun unless he possessed at least an elementary knowledge of the game he sought. Yet this is precisely what a majority of anglers do, with regard to fish. Fishes depend exclusively on their senses for safety against the wiles of the fisherman, and yet he uses, for the most part, entirely what is provided for him in the shape of tackle, and does as he is told in the arrangement of baits, and his own comportment. Verily, such an one has usually too great a reward, but he

(7)

is no angler. In these days of competition, it is necessary for the true angler to excel, and patient observation, added to the experience of others, is demanded. The more the angler becomes a naturalist, the more he finds out the beauties and weaknesses of his quarry, and the greater the enjoyment of the craft. The more he observes the various powers employed by these beautiful animals, the more skilful does he become. It is with this firm conviction that I offer the result of many years of observation of the habits of fish, with especial reference to their senses. They are particularly necessary to the fly-fisherman who aspires to be worthy of the name, for his is the most artistic, as well as the most difficult, of all the varied methods of fishing. My remarks are, however, intended, above all, to be suggestive rather than conclusive.

I.—VISION.

The faculty of vision is probably the most important of all to the fish—at all events, to the fish that come within the ken of the sportsman. Blind fish exist in subterranean waters—for example, those found in the Mammoth Cave, Kentucky—and in the case of fishes feeding in deep water, the existence of barbules or feelers is, without question, for the purpose of assisting the vision. I can say nothing about the methods providing for the sustenance of these blind subterranean fish. Probably they exist on stationary food of some kind ; so far as the present purpose is concerned they may be dismissed from further consideration. Trout, and other sport-fish, unquestionably make great use of their eyes, and it is very surprising to what state of education nearly all our fresh water fishes may and do arrive, under the pursuance of the angler, or general fisherman.

The formation of the eye of the fish does not materially differ, one species from another, among the angler's fishes. The cornea is somewhat flat in sectional outline, and the shape, or, so to speak, the ground plan, is virtually similar in save the European grayling (*S. thymallus*). The pupil of the eye of this fish is oval instead of circular—the oval of the plover's egg rather than that of the hen, being sharper than a true oval at one end. The apex of this sharp end is pointed toward the upper part of the head, tailward, giving the fish a somewhat sinister appearance. What purpose this particular configuration serves I do not know, but one thing is certain : The visual ability of the grayling is equal, if not superior, to that of the trout, as is proved by its rising, often from a great depth, to the fly. I notice, also, that the normal waiting position of this fish is inclined toward the water's surface instead of being horizontal, as is usually the case with trout. This being so, the greater mass of the rays of direct sunlight would fall on the forward part of the eye, and I offer it as a conjecture, based on the law of development, that this, continued through generations, has evolved the peculiar shape. The grayling of this country, though apparently similar in every other respect, does not exhibit the peculiarity referred to.

It is a general law, observable through the whole range of animal life possessing vision, that the eye is peculiarly adapted to the medium through which (and to the manner in which) it receives the light. The more closely we look into this truth, the more apparent and wonderful is the adaptability. Indeed, these premises are truisms, and would not need repetition did not we so habitually forget that design is the key to all the natural phenomena around us. Admitting this, it follows that the structure of the eye of a fish and its position are admirably adapted for seeing in a denser medium than air with great precision and certainty. Observation ratifies this conclusion in its entirety. The vitreous and crystalline humors of the organ are not different from those of other animals. The muscles moving the body of the eye are large and permit great freedom, and the power of contraction and expansion of the irides is also distinct and pronounced. In air, this latter feature is, indeed, very noticeable in the case of some fishes, and the angler has only to accurately measure the breadth of the pupil of such fish in shaded water, and compare this with the measurement of the same after the fish has lain in full sunlight a few moments, to be at once forcibly impressed by the fact. The position of the orbit also needs a word of comment. In fish which readily and constantly rise and descend, to feed, it is placed so as to command a large area around ; in fact, as large as in the nature of the creature is possible. In such as chiefly rise to their prey, as the pikes, it is placed quite near the top of the head. In the barbel (*Cyprinus barbus*) and gudgeon (*Gobio fluviatilis*) the converse obtains. In the trout, however, the orbit is more central, and the broad visual grasp of this fish, therefore, is one of the reasons why it, in due time, becomes so wary and so capable of protecting itself against its arch enemy—man. A pike cannot possibly see its ventral fin ; a trout undoubtedly could, if it felt so disposed. On the other hand, a pike could see much further behind and backward than a trout. Indeed, the practice of up-stream fly-fishing, to which I record my own attachment, is based on the theory that the trout cannot see behind it but an exceedingly short distance.

Taking the trout as a fish not likely to seriously vary in regard to its faculties and their possibilities because of habitat, let us endeavor to ascertain the range of this power of vision, both in the light of what has been said, and what follows. First, one small but important fact has to be noted as bearing collaterally but interestingly on the subject. The fish is hard to frighten by means of any object it sees in water only, as separate and distinct from its cause or connection in air, if such exist. To make this plainer : If an object be presented so that another person, besides the presentor, can see its reception by the fish (himself unseen), that person will notice it seldom happens that the trout retires or darts away unless actually or positively touched—say with the point of a rod. Even then, so that the impact be gentle, he is not alarmed, and this fact is taken advantage of by the "groping" poacher of Europe, who gently places his hand under the trout—lying with its eyes buried in the weeds thinking itself secure, as does the ostrich when it buries its head in the sand—and lifts it suddenly to the bank. Be the object presented a stone or a fly, so that its connection with the arch enemy of fishdom be not discovered, the fish fears not. Its brilliant, infallible visual faculty has apprehended the innocuousness of the object, *per se*, and no fear is aroused.

Try the experiment with the operator in full sight.

What a difference in the result! The trout vanishes like a lightning flash, and be very certain that he will not again present himself to be "fooled" with, however good your intentions. "Of course he won't, and what of it ?" you say. "But why," I ask, "did he bolt ?" "Let bears and lions growl and fight, it is their nature to," you reply, quoting the saintly Watts. That might satisfy the feminine mind, and be absolutely conclusive to a majority of the masculine persuasion, but I don't propose to let the reader, who has followed thus far, off so easily. We ought to look a little deeper into this apparently transparent matter, and I want the patient reader's close attention.

Now, water, if clear, is a particularly pleasant medium through which to view its contents, even with the human eye. Of course, I do not quite know how fish feel about it, but I do know that if I am watching the movements of an aquatic insect—be it water-flea or water-devil (larva of the dragon-fly), I do not choose, as the best way, to gaze at it through the air into the water. No, I endeavor to immerse my eyes—I've slipped in head first more than once doing this—and thus I get a more distinct and clearer view than if I only held my head just above in the air. This is a "dodge" taught me by the Reverend J. G. Wood, than whom there is no better "minute philosopher" in the world. The fact is that the interposition of two *media*—air and water—between the eyes and the object have a tendency to distort or render the image indefinite. The human eye is perfectly fitted for seeing in either a dense or rare medium, but not through both so well as through one separately. I do not claim that fish can see indifferently well in either, of course, but rather from the fact that it sees so excellently in water, and from the comparative fixity of the irides, I would argue that the image it perceives through water and air is ill-defined, blurred, uncertain, and altogether, in most cases, grotesque and awesome to the piscine intelligence. *Ergo*, the fish is startled by any moving object.

A well-known optical law, which does not affect the main argument, must now be referred to. Ronald, in "The Fly-Fisher's Entomology," gives it and, as I do not think that its importance is sufficiently recognized, I reproduce it with grateful acknowledgements: When Mr. A. B., situated upon a certain eminence at a given distance from a fish, which is near the bottom of the water, looks over the edge of a bank, in its direction, he might, if unacquainted with the laws of refraction, imagine that neither the fish, nor any other fish below the line of his direct vision, could see him ; whereas, the fish could see A. B. by means of the pencil of light, bent or refracted at the surface of the water, and the image of A. B. would appear in the eye of the fish, shortened and transferred to a much higher point. The fish, in fact, could see the whole of the man round or over the corner of the bank by the aid of the water above it ; but if the surface of the water should be about as low as the fish's eye, then he could not see any part of A. B.'s figure, because a straight or unrefracted pencil of light would be obstructed by the bank.

Increasing obliquity in pencils of light falling from an object upon a surface of water is accompanied by still more rapidly increasing refraction, but the distinctness with which the object is seen increases in inverse proportion.

The bending or refraction which a pencil of light, falling very obliquely on the surface of the water, undergoes before arriving at the eye of a fish, is sufficient to produce very great indistinctness and distortion of the image of the man formed in his eye.

Long before a pencil of light becomes horizontal, it will not enter the water at all; consequently, although the fish may see the upper part of the man wading, he will do so very indistinctly and in a new position, because the pencil will be very much refracted; he will not see the middle part of the man at all, because the pencil does not enter the water, and he will see, probably, his legs in the clear water, because there is neither refraction nor obstruction to prevent him. So that the figure of the man will be, in the eye of the fish, cut in two portions, separated from each other by a long unsubstantial interval.

The lessons to be drawn from these theories are, briefly, three. 1st. A low bank on the level of the water is a great advantage to the fisherman. 2d. The wader has a great advantage over the bank fisher. 3d. It is of great advantage to fish up stream, wading when the fish are heading in that direction. "Observe," says Ronald, "that fish cannot see behind them; all optics forbid it." To which I add an emphatic endorsement.

But the trout has, probably, in addition, another and more subtle reason why my presence, or that of a waving rod, is a signal for taking his leave—standing not on the order of his going, but going at once ; and this is an instinct—intuitive, I believe—which, apart from the direct teachings of the senses, informs him that certain creatures are his enemies. I have seen a stream literally boiling with rising trout, one moment, and the next, as a weird, ghostly heron sailed slowly over it, you would swear it did not possess a fish, so quickly had they ceased rising, and so instantly had they hidden themselves. Yet, when a flock of rooks had passed just as close only a few minutes before, though they ceased rising for a few seconds during the actual flight, there was no general stampede. Explain that circumstance if you can, gentle reader, on any hypothesis than that the fish recognized the foe of their race, instinctively. Once I caught a kingfisher in a trap set just over the water of my tank of young, feeding trout, and did not release its body, seeing it was dead, ere I proceeded to cast to the fish the victuals I had brought. Now, on other occasions previously, these little, domesticated *farios* would rise *en masse* to the chopped meat and meal, on which I was wont to feed them, for I accustomed them to be fed a little at a time but often, and they rather regarded my presence in a friendly spirit. On this occasion, however, their alacrity was turned to a startled, restless demeanor, which is easily detected by the watchful fish-breeder and lover. Was the kingfisher the cause of the uneasiness? I won't assert so much, but I have a private belief, built up and strengthened by many trivial observations, of which these two are but samples. "*Credat Judæus Apella!*" you mutter. Nathless, however, I doubt not, oh, sceptic ! there are more things between heaven and earth than are dreamt of in your philosophy, and this mysterious instinct may be one of them.

Again, why is it that no matter how quiet I stand, the fish that has stopped rising a few yards down stream will not rise again if I remain where he can see me, though I be as still as the Great Pyramid, or anything else that is mighty quiet? Of course I am referring to a much fished, clear river.

I can only reply that the evils of taking the imitation fly, without due circumspection, have somehow been inculcated as an experimental lesson—*experientia docet*, we are taught every hour of our lives—so often that at last it has become a part of the fishy nature, and is transmitted hereditarily. And does not that sum up what instinct is? Denuded of all the elaborations and jargon of metaphysics, is not instinct the result of successive experiences which have become actual, permanent impressions on the brain? Some may smile at this, but let me ask what makes the young wild duck, just in the act of breaking from its shell, hustle this off in great trepidation, as I stoop to pick it up, and break for the water as if a horde of miniature fiends were pursuing it? An inherent instinct derived from the parents is the reply, for it certainly was not acquired from bygone personal experiences.

And I doubt not that the necessity for the finest tackle and closest of imitations of the natural insect on the much fished streams of England is due to a like progressive evolving education (which I may as well refer to in this section on "Vision," though it concerns all the other observant perceptions). The earliest work on

angling in the English language is that of the fair Dame
Berners (1496), and it is too practical internally for us to
doubt that the drawings and descriptions she gives
of tackle are, indeed, representations of what caught fish
in her day.   Yet an angler would be mad to attempt the
use of such rough implements now, either in this or any
other country.

And further, on virgin streams, which still exist,
though rarely, the comparative tameness and unsophist-
ication of the fish argue that the march of intellect—
or as a " too, too utter" Boston writer terms it, the
" march of cephalization "—in a comparative sense applies to fish as to all other animals.   The ancient angler,
whose rod was a sturdy oak—

> "His line a cable that in storms ne'er broke,
>   His hook was baited with a dragon's tail,
>   He sat upon a rock and bobbed for whale,"

—this man would probably scorn the gossamer gut and
tiny, accurately imaged fly used on clear, hard-fished
streams.   Yet hundreds of fly-fishers will bear me wit-
ness that the latter are indispensable.   Probably this extreme refinement is not yet so absolutely necessary in
this country, but the day is not far distant when it will
be, and many good anglers of my acquaintance are even
now embracing it as a means to more invariable good
sport on clear streams.

One palpable result of this education of trout " on the
other side " is the general adoption of the dry fly up-
stream fishing.   The angler stalks his fish from behind
as he lies head up stream and, drying the fly by means of
a couple or three flips backward and forward in the air,

he casts it just before the rising fish and lets it float, taking care that no move is imparted to the lure as it rides downward on the stream. If the imitation is a good one the fish takes it ; if bad, he pronounces on it adversely. Now let it be understood that it is emphatically well-nigh impossible to get good sport on an English chalk stream, especially among the "big uns," in any other way whatsoever—barring bait fishing. Let this latter be Anathema ; Maranatha ! always and forever where the fly can be used.

" Why can the fish be caught in no other way ? " you ask. Because, I reply, this style places the lure before the fish in the nearest possible approach to its natural way of sailing down stream after falling on the water or rising from it. " But," you object, "there are no imitations of the struggling insect in this style !" I deny that the water insect does struggle. Those flies whose previous larval existence has been in the water are not afraid of their natural element, and sail down with erect wings (they chiefly belong to the *neuroptera*) and immovably out-spread legs, with majestic nonchalance. So does the imitation, and hence the rise of the fish. The land flies certainly do struggle like the fly in your milk jug, and the down-stream angler who jerks and jiggers his flies to make them lively, may be thankful that he has that one small piece of nature to be faithful to. It just saves his credit to be like something, but the flies he imitates are in a miserable minority.

The education of the eye in individual trout can occasionally be met with advanced to a degree actually astounding. This is chiefly found in connection with fish who have passed the grand climacteric and are getting old and learned and, in many cases, lean as well. Learning seems to render mankind lean also, and the "sock-dolager" of the stream rarely maintains his aldermanic outline when his education is at the meridian. His seven or eight summers have filled him full of suspicion, and he knows precisely the difference between even the most artfully imitated fly and the real Simon Pure. Before now I have caught specimens of the fly that such a fish has actually been taking, and by the aid of the magnifying lens and the closest study, have selected the exact colors for the imitation—nay, more, the exact size and shape of the insect has been duplicated. And to what purpose ? Deftly have I, with throbbing pulse, cast that fly over the grand old patriarch poised in mid-stream ready for any emergency, only to see him sail calmly toward it, examine it, and then turn tail on it, saying, just as plainly as if he spoke in the eloquent vernacular of the glorious English language, "See you d—d first." Ugh! the intellectual accomplishments of the more than one "beastie" of that kind make me weary when I think of them !

I particularly recall one old fellow that annoyed me for three mortal years, till I became almost monomaniac. He took up his quarters close to the buttress of a rustic bridge which spanned the stream, and in clear, bright weather you could easily watch his movements from daylight till dark if you had a mind to do so. Just so long as I would blow, from a pea-shooter, fat, large, green drakes, so long would he come up with his huge whip lips smacking out, plop ! and take them. On the other hand, just as soon as I put a hook through a couple of the live insects and lowered them to him, even using—quite against the rule in this style of " dapping "—the finest of gut and a small hook, would he retire like a duchess from Queen Victoria, backward—into deeper water. The next minute I would see him going for other natural flies. Now, this fish unquestionably knew and saw the gut and hook, and connected them with me. I don't see how we can avoid that conclusion. And it occurred continually during the three years; try what I would, he would not be tempted. At the end of the third season, however, I determined to get him out, for I could see that age had rendered him lank and thin, and during the ensuing winter he would probably have become a spawn-eater. Still, I venerated the "varmint" too much to net him. I wanted to deceive him somehow; to get even with his transcendent wile, and at last screwed my courage to the "sticking point" of "foxing" him, as Charles Kingsley would say. This is what I did, and it succeeded: Morning after morning, for a week or so, I fed him on bread—of which trout are very fond in some waters, by the bye—and he seemed to relish that diet with extreme gusto. One fatal morning I rigged up a single hook on fine gut, and after he had one or two boluses of bread as sweeteners, I floated one down with the hook in it. He rose and took it—chung! went the line as I struck the keen steel into his rough old jaw. There never was a madder fish on this side of the Styx, but I landed him. And so he died at the weight of three and three-quarter pounds avoirdupois, with eye undimmed, and natural force unabated.

Not only is this education of the eye of old fishes noticeable in reference to daylight fishing, but it is equally so in reference to the use of such night flies as the various white moths, which are very deadly on dark evenings if used properly—and that, amongst the largest and best fish for the most part. The capacity of the trout's eye for making the most of the scarce light of night may be greater than we know, owing to our difficulty of estimating it in the dark. I never, however, noticed that there was anything specially favorable in the fact that the moth was white, as one might suppose— sport being equally good in my experience when the Fetid Brown or Cinnamon flies were used in place of the moth. Besides, it is probable that each and all look equally dark when outlined against the sky, and, therefore, the faculty which enables these patriarchs of the stream to secure their prey at night in the dark as well, or nearly so as in the light, may, I submit, be fairly presumed to arise from the education of the eye which, as we know in the case of some astronomers, is possible to a very exalted degree as the result of persistent and long continued training.

Although the whole of the foregoing screed is intended to throw light (howsoever dimly) on the *rationale* of the taking of the fly in its character as an imitation of the natural food-insect, I am aware that it does not touch the fact that trout will take fancy flies of any and all conceivable patterns, which are like nothing in the "heavens above, the earth beneath, or the waters under the earth." I have even known trout to rise at Mr. H. Cholmondeley Pennell's three typical nondescripts, which is, on the fish's part, piling the Pelion of idiocy on the Ossa of absurdity. Then, again, the salmon takes that poem of color, a salmon fly, when the natural minnow fly or worm will not lure him. Why? Is it sheer wantonness akin to that which prompts the omnivorous appetite of the ostrich or camel, who swallow with relish anything from a door-key to a newspaper, or are the fish, as Sir Bedivere,

> " Like a girl
> Valuing the giddy pleasure of the eyes "

over the gem-like insect, counterfeit? The man who says, honestly, " I don't know," is to be respected. Respect me, therefore, oh! gentle reader, for I am ignorant in this matter. Perchance the fish see in the fancy fly some of the qualities which are the quintessence of delight and piquancy to its fishy palate. Suppose a boy came across a fruit, hanging on a tree, within reach, having the odor of strawberry and pine-apple, the juicy, luscious appearance of pear and peach, together with the creamy pulp of the banana—in short, possessing all the sublimated qualities of the most delicious of imaginable fruits, to the eye and nose—could we wonder at him for plucking and attempting to eat it, even if the taste were ashes—like that of Dead Sea apples? Indeed, the " gardener Adam and his wife," did just that thing. Perhaps, I say, the trout and salmon find themselves in an analogous position. Imagine one of the Silver Doctor's or Parmachene Belle's, made by Orvis, floating over a *blasé* trout, the sunlight rippling through its many-hued fibers, and lighting it up until its appearance excels that of the apparel of an Eastern queen, and further remember that

the trout cannot put forth a hand to grasp the glittering
trifle ; it has, like a baby, one universal receptacle only
—its mouth—whereby to test the quality of all comfits,—
then, I say, ask yourself where is the wonder that the
wary fish loses caution in the sensuous pleasure of the
momentary acquisition, bites and ends its life, not ignominiously, but fighting to the last. I am not joking.
This is the only explanation I can offer after a quarter
of a century's wondering.

II.—HEARING.

Hearing is the power of perceiving vibration, whether
possessed by a land or water animal, and as abundant
evidence exists that fish are sensible of vibration, there
can be no excuse for saying that they cannot hear. Hear,
they do, and, in their way, most readily, but not in the
same way as a creature in the air.

I need hardly remind the reader, that the ear of a
human being is a structure of excelling adaptability
equally fitted to appreciate the melodies and harmonies
of a Mendelsohn, or to the stunning monotone of the
thunder clap, and to convey, according to the degrees of
refinement, definite impressions of each to the mind.
This organ in man is also divided into two sections,
broadly distinguished as the outer and inner—external
and internal ear. The former of these is wanting in
fish, and as an apparatus for the collection and magnifi-
cation of sound, as it is in air, is not required in water,
the denser medium, its absence is precisely what we
should expect to find. In place of this, a nerve running
from the base of each scale to a large ganglion in the

head, allows the fish to perceive vibration instantly from the whole of its surface, as well as immediately from the outer part of the head. The trout is specially furnished in this way, and the interior mechanism of the ear in all fishes is very beautifully adapted to their requirements. The curious oolith, or brain ivory, possessed by nearly all fishes, forms the bones guarding this aural development, and sometimes these are of exceeding delicacy and beauty. In the loaches there is a connection between the ear and the air cavity, situated in the anterior part of the head, which may be supplementary to their impaired sight in daylight, and the same peculiarity is noticeable in the *Cobitis Barbatula,* a small loach of English streams, and the *Cottus gobio,* a bull-head. Both these are almost exclusively night feeders.

Sound travels in air at the rate—roughly—of eleven hundred feet per second ; in water, accurate experiments fix it at over five thousand feet in that space of time. When quite a youngster I satisfied myself of its extreme rapidity and the great conducting power of water, on several occasions, in the following way : The fishermen of the Thames use an iron-shod pole, termed a ryepeck, to fix the punt when fishing, and this experiment was made : A friend took a boat and rowed down on a long clear reach of water to the end of a measured mile. I remained at the starting point, divested of my clothes. As he got to the end of the mile I stepped into the water, which was about up to my armpits, with a small red flag in my hand, and as soon as he saw my head disappear under the surface it was agreed he should ram the iron down, and I was to exhibit the flag on hearing the sound. Well,

I need not say that no exact result accrued; but one or two wholesome lessons, certainly, were taught me. One was— and this was just then most valuable, I being the son of a professional fisherman—that it was a great mistake to ram a pole in the river to fasten the boat at all, for the sound was startingly clear, though made a mile away, and the grating of the gravel and iron was louder than in air even to my ears, which, it must be borne in mind, were fitted rather for sounds in air. The water seems to act as a sort of microphone—indeed, magnifying the sound, considering the distance, of course.

I do not believe that sound made in air is heard at all under water. The experiments of Ronald favor this opinion, and of course my own are, to my mind, conclusive, or I should not give in my belief so sweepingly. Dr. Henshall ("Book of Black Bass"), however, thinks differently. Let us see how the assertions of these two redoubtable sportsmen look side by side :

Dr. Henshall, "Book of Black Bass," page 184.

"I have frequently observed that fish exhibit symptoms of great fright or alarm at the report of fire-arms, or other loud noises, and be scared and dart away at the sound of the human voice or the barking of a dog, when the fish could not see the originators of the noises."

Alfred Ronald, "Fly-Fisher's Entomology," page 7.

"In order that we might be enabled to ascertain the truth of the common assertion (viz.:) that fish can hear voices in conversation on the banks of a stream, my friend, the Reverend Mr. Brown, of Gratwich, and myself selected for close observation a trout poised about six inches deep in the water, whilst a third gentleman, who was situated behind the fishing house—*i. e.*, diametrically opposite to the side where the fish was, fired off a gun. The possibility of the flash being seen by the fish was thus wholly prevented and the report produced not the slightest effect upon him.

"The second barrel was then fired; still he remained immovable, evincing not the slightest symptom of having heard the report. This experiment was often repeated, and precisely similar results obtained. Neither could I, or other persons, ever awaken symptoms of alarm in fishes near the boat by shouting to them in our loudest tones, although our distance from them sometimes did not exceed six feet. * * * It is sufficient to know that the above trout had no ears to hear either the voices or the gun, and I firmly believe that the zest which friendly chat often imparts to the exercise of our captivating art need never be marred by an apprehension that sport will be impaired thereby."

Who shall decide when doctors disagree?

Speaking of firing off a gun to test the hearing of trout reminds me of the only incident I can call to mind which apparently contradicts the conclusions reached by Ronald.

It occurred on one of Queen Victoria's birthdays. Windsor Park, England, possesses a beautiful ornamental lake named Virginia Water, and located on this is a miniature frigate of twenty-one guns—five-pounders, I think. On each royal birthday it is customary to fire a salute with these, and on the occasion of which I speak the small fish, roach, etc., were in shoals of hundreds of thousands near the surface of the water surrounding the vessel. This is not uncommon on a still, fine day—the lake being so overwhelmingly full of the little fellows. The salute was fired, gun after gun, at minute intervals, and the vibratory reverberating boom seemed to startle the small fish, and all around the vessel the water broke into ripples, as if stirred by wind, as each report was fired. Now this seems as if the fish heard the sound and didn't approve of it ; but if we look deeper, it is possible—nay, probable —that the mechanical shock of sound was strong enough to make itself felt in the layer of water which is most laden with atmospheric air—namely, the top or surface.

Of course the vibration of the vessel itself from the recoil may have been the true cause, and is the solution of the matter I most favor. Shortly, my experience is that you may whistle, laugh, sing and talk—I except " cussing "—but you must not stamp your feet in the boat or on the bank if you desire to capture trout.

Against my opinion that fish cannot hear sounds in air is David Foster's ("Scientific Angler") funny reference to a friend who always took a musical box to sit on, and this he set going while he fished. A veritable Sybarite in angling like this ought to catch a good string. A far greater example, however, of different opinion is that which credits carp coming to the call of a bell or whistle at feeding time. I doubt not that such instances are true—that the fish did respond. In the range of angling literature I could pick out a dozen recorded instances of such docility and obedience.

"Then," says the impartial reader, "you have contradicted yourself—the fish *can* hear sounds coming from the air." Let us make haste slowly, fair sir, and, prithee, let me put a few questions to the writers of these records of clever fish. First, Mr. Historian, were you positively there when the incident occurred? Did the fish-feeder not feed at a regular time, and did he not walk in an unguarded, ordinary manner to his fish ponds? Did they not see him coming or hear his step? The answers enclose the gist of the question. Why, at Denham Fishery, in England, I have seen a herd of thousands of *fontinalis* trout, up to three and four pounds, following the proprietor, General Gerald Goodlake, as he walked up the bank. These fish were fed regularly once a day with chopped, cooked horse flesh. But there was no calling in the matter. They heard the heavy tread of this Saul among men, and saw his mighty form and remembered the old, large check suit in which he always fed his pets. Nothing more. Foster, in the "Scientific Angler," states that "no noise which does not occasion a vibration of the element which they inhabit reaches them;" and with this opinion I fully agree.

III.—TASTE.

Authorities of all kinds agree in denying that fish possess a very discriminating palate. I grant that there are degrees of discriminating power, and that the voracious fish are but slightly endowed with them to any nicety ; but then, are there not degrees in connection with the human gastronomist ? Would not the blubber-eating Greenlander prefer his gross meal to the *paté de foie gras* of the Parisian *gourmand?* " A question not to be asked," as Falstaff would say, and I have myself met a specimen of the *genus homo,* who would disdain the juicy steak and dine off bacon-fat in preference. If there is a lack of delicacy among men in this particular, why not among fishes ? But is there a lack of particularity which would indicate an absolute absence of taste in the inhabitants of the water ? Let us see.

The pikes will take anything when hungry, you will say, from a lead sinker to a red cork float. Yes, I admit, that if you meet him on the aqueous highway, and you possess a spark of bright metal about you, he will assail you. It is, as Tennyson puts it, " Sense at war with soul." The fish jumps out on a spoon in the hope that when he crushes it, it will be fish-like, and so meat for him. I say he will do this on impulse, but try a fish-bait that is not fresh, and though he may seize it he will never swallow it, no matter how ravenous he may be. Again, in England, there is an olive, mucous coated, flat-fish, termed the tench, which for some reason (some say gratitude !) the fish will not touch. Though Esox Lucius will grow fat on every other member of the family of the Cyprinidæ, or carps, yet you may fish all day in a lake or river thronged with pike, using tench, and you will not catch a pike. Again, with a golden fish (*Cyprinus auratus*) I can catch four times more pike than with any other bait.

Next in point of favor comes the dace or dare, and next,
the gudgeon. Says honest Jack Falstaff, "Why, if a
dace be a bait for an old pike, may I not grab him?"
So, from these irrefragable facts, even the pike "fell,
tyrant of the watery plain," though he be, does, possess
a sense quite worthy of the appellation—taste.

And now, in regard to trout, which chiefly concerns us
here—though a passing consideration of other fish is emi-
nently useful in order to lead to a wide comprehension of
the subject—who shall assert its lack of discrimination
in matters gastronomic? Can it not tell the difference
between the flavor of a spent May fly and a female Green
Drake full of luscious, creamy eggs? Or, between the
various kind of flies, which at different times may be
upon the water. When the beautiful Blue Dun is rising,
I have seen that it alone is taken, to the absolute ex-
clusion of other flies; yet, the trout are hungry, or why
do they feed, and if they do not discriminate, why not
feed on everything before them?

The meaning of the word taste requires exposition in
this connection. First—It indicates a perception of
pleasant or unpleasant tastes in foods or liquids conveyed
to the mouth. Second—The sense of taste is in inti-
mate connection with the stomach, and that which
violently disagrees with this organ is usually unpleasant
and rejected instinctively.

Here are two instances of the antipathies of European
fresh water fishes, which cannot be accounted for in the
absence of a sense of taste in the fish:

(1.) Roach (*Leuciscus rutilus*) are often taken in great
numbers by a bait made of flour paste. In the full tide

of catching fish, if the experiment of squeezing a few drops of tobacco juice into the paste from the end of a wet cigar is tried, not one fish more will take that paste. Expert roach fishermen never smoke when fishing, for this reason.

(2.) Barbel (a gregarious ground feeder), are often caught one after the other, as rapidly as it is possible to reel in with the fresh lob worm, (garden worm). If you throw in a handful of worms that are dead, you will put them off their feed for that day. A single fact such as these is worth a cartload of mere theories. It proves incontestably that fish possess discriminating palates.

The tasting powers of trout were made the object of special experiments by Ronald. He projected, by means of a blow-pipe, house flies to his trout, and plastered various strong condiments, such as mustard and pepper, over them. He says the fish took them indifferently. Now, it would be interesting to know how much of the spices remained on the flies as they sailed down the water after going through the air from the blow pipe? And it is fair to presume that they would not be covered so completely as to hide their identity as flies. Howbeit, it is also said that a large bee was thrown to a trout, which he took; but he rejected a wasp—didn't relish the "business end" of him, perhaps!

Of course, I do not assert that fish have the sense of taste in the same perfection as warm-blooded animals, but I contend they exhibit like and dislike in a lesser degree certainly, but by no means in a dissimilar way. Especially would I insist that the carp family, with their soft, palatal tongues, possess it in a high degree. The large, massive molar teeth crush and masticate, in the throat of them all, whatever food is passed, and it would seem extraordinary to me if by sight alone this "fox of the water" builds up his oft-times colossal form and fat.

IV.—SMELL.

I think, after what I have seen of the manifestations of this sense in fishes that it does not exist in such a high state of development as does even taste. The sense of smell in air depends on the perception of minute particles thrown off by the odorate body. Hence, the necessity for a refined sense of smell does not exist in water, for it cannot be supposed that particles of any object could diffuse themselves in the denser medium with the rapidity and completeness with which they do it in air.

Nevertheless, fishes possess nostrils, though these have no communication with the gills or mouth cavity. I remember that Mr. Frank Buckland passed a fine bristle far into the head of a thirty-six pound pike (caught by my late father in Windsor Great Park) he was casting, in my presence some years ago, from each of the small orifices which extend in a row on either side of the muzzle.

Pollutions of the water are avoided by fish ; and when some poisonous chemical refuse was once thrown into a stream under my care, I saw many fish throw themselves out upon the banks to avoid encountering the horrible corroding flood. This, however, might have been due to an impending sense of suffocation, and the pain consequent on the cauterizing effect the poison had on the *branchiæ*. Fish are not adverse to even a large amount of sewage if the latter be fresh, but putrid fæcal matter is a horrible and unqualified destroyer of all water-courses whatsoever, and should be utterly and relentlessly reprobated by all interested in the preservation of fish for food and sport.

So far as trout are concerned, the sense of smell does not appear superiorly developed, in comparison with other fishes. I am not willing to believe that this sense exists in a state of higher refinement in fish as compared with ourselves, and, therefore, as we cannot detect any particular odor in the food of this species (except in such flies as the Fetid Brown, or Cinnamon fly, *limnephilus stigmaticus*, and a few others), it is fair to presume that the trout do not. It is true that the ancient works on angling frequently speak of oils and unguents for the attraction of fish, but I never could find they were of any use, and I have tried scores of recipes. Some time since, a firm in England began selling "stinking Gladwin" as an infallible enticer of fish. I used some, and was disappointed, as I deserved to be. If trout or any other fish perceive the whereabouts of food from a distance, it is owing to their microscopic keenness of sight in perceiving the tiny detached fragments flowing from it. These they will follow up and find—as is well-known to the still fisherman who has ground baited—by taste and sight rather than smell. The latter sense, in fish, I am inclined to place amongst the impossibilities, though I have, somewhat "Hibernically," to use an euphemism, devoted quite a space to its consideration.

V.—FEELING.

This sense is well developed in all the angler's fishes, but varies in its development. This variation appears to me to depend on or is adjusted to the degrees of development manifested by the other senses, especially that of vision. For instance: The pike (*Esox Lucius*) is an exceedingly sharp-sighted fish. If you fix your eyes on his as he lies, *perdu*, sunning himself in the water, you may so chain his attention as to allow of another person placing a wire noose around his body and hauling him out. But if your eyes waver, or the gaze be removed, like lightning he is gone. I have done this hundreds of times when snaring pike from a trout stream, and mention it chiefly to prove his quick sight. Now you may catch him with a "flight" or "gang" of four or five hooks, belonging to some previous angler, stuck in his jaw. I have taken him with a lead-bound hook already fixed in his maw, and have lost a hook on a pike and in thirty minutes captured the fish with the tackle hanging to him. This does not look much like evidence that fish suffer pain. Indeed, the extremely dogmatic Mr. Cholmondeley Pennell, says, in the "Fisherman's Magazine:" "In sober seriousness, it has been proved over and over again—on evidence strong enough to hang a man—or what has been considered still more difficult, to build a church—the organization of a fish, which is a cold-blooded animal, does not admit of its feeling pain." Then there is the grayling, which I believe to be one of the sharpest sighted of fishes ; he will come again and again to a fly, even after being pricked by the hook, and who has not caught a trout with somebody else's fly in its jaw ?

Such fish, it is true, feel but little pain in the process of capture, but I feel certain the matter is far different with others possessing softer mouths and greater development of nerve-perceptive power. Nevertheless, I lay it down as a *dictum* borne out by examination—why, I do not know, of course—that the greater the refinement and power of sight, the less is that of feeling or perception of pain on being caught. The connection between the two is not apparent. These are the facts, however. Of course, I am now only referring to the jaws and head generally. When I come to consider perception in the other parts of a fish's body, the circumstances vary somewhat, and the sense of sight does not exhibit the same bearing.

I opine that in those fish which feed in deep places, and collect their aliment chiefly from the soil, the act of capture by hook is painful. Most of these possess barbules, and of all fresh water fish, the cat-fish and its relations furnish the most striking examples. Next to these the carp family provide ample illustrations. One English fish—the barbel—to which I have before referred, gives point to my meaning perfectly. The fish grows to some six or seven pounds, though its average size does not exceed two and a half, and they congregate in large shoals. Its feelers, or barbules, are four in number, and in a fish of several pounds are quite half an inch in length. On dissecting these, they are found to abound in nerve filaments, somewhat like the trunk of an elephant, and there is a very free movement. Doubtless the dissection of the feelers of the cat-fish would reveal a similar and probably greater development of nerve fiber, and this fact is sufficient presumption of exquisite perceptive power.

So, also, the carp is gifted in a similar manner, and the daintiness of the fish is proverbial, whilst the loach (*Cobitis barbatula*), which lies under stones during the day-time and feeds best on the darkest night, has, in proportion, the most plenteous organs of perception of all. It has six barbules, and if you are so fortunate as to see the little fish feeding in the shady corner of an aquarium, you will observe the investigating movements of the tentacles in a state of great activity. These organs—who can doubt it—are precisely analogous to those of the feline tribe, namely the whiskers, and even to the fingers of the *genus homo*.

I apprehend, also, that this perceptive faculty is in correspondence with the development of the soft parts of the jaw and their neighboring processes ; hence, the bony pike cares little for the hook, whilst no mortal ever yet caught a carp with a lost hook in its jaw, or a barbel or a chub ! (*Leuciscus cephalus*).

The perception of sensation in reference to other parts of the body of fishes is an obscure subject, and I shall detail what I have observed, drawing this inference only—that in proportion as the scales are small, the sensitiveness of the cuticle increases. Reasoning thus, we would therefore expect to find the eel the most highly gifted of all, seeing that its scales are microscopical in their minuteness. Nor are we disappointed. The eel will remain quite unconscious of your presence in the bright sunlight, "like an owl in a holly-bush," as the saying is; but gently touch it with the tip of your rod, and see the celerity with which it undulates away. The trout does not resent the touch of the hand if it does not see you; but if, as is asserted by Professor Cope, in Dr. Henshall's "Book of the Black Bass," it hears through its scales, its perceptions must, in this regard, be exquisitely delicate.

That fish feel exquisite pain on the wounding of their bodies, I cannot doubt. The barbarous method of bass and other fishing, which compels the passing of a hook under the skin of a minnow, shows by the shudders and quivers of agony in the luckless bait how fearfully it suffers. Don't talk to me about "reflex action" of the muscles in this case! Again, the pestilent salmon disease, which, like a loathsome leprosy, first covers up the eyes and nostrils of the fish with a fungoid growth (*Saprolegnia ferax*) and then spreads over the entire body, often causes the hapless fish to dash itself against the rocks, or leap out on shore, under the sense of the intolerable irritation. Again, the presence of internal as well as external parasites, are particularly a source of pain to trout. I have several times dissected trout which had previously appeared unhealthy and dark-colored, to find them infested with either the larval tape-worm (*ligula digamma of Creplin*), or a liver fluke similiar to that of sheep. Indeed, the subject of fish diseases is a very interesting one, and quite worth more investigation, apart from its bearing on the question of pain.

CHAPTER II.

PRACTICAL FLY-FISHING.

Practical anglers, as a rule, are not reading men. Your "reading" man—he who with unfeigned delight reads carefully every angling work that comes in his way; weighs the *pros* and *cons* of the controversy "up *versus* down stream fishing," "dry" *versus* "wet" fly, "eyed" *versus* "ordinary" hook, "typical" *versus* "imitation" flies, etc., etc., is commonly not a very practical angler, and I firmly believe that the really successful fishermen who have derived solid benefit from the many beautiful works published on fishing are in the minority. I am forced to this conclusion after a lengthened experience of anglers and their ways. The fact is, that literary style and finish is usually incompatible with concrete and pithy direction and explanation. One can hardly put polish and style into a book of prescriptions, and yet this is really the sort of thing that the practical man needs when he wants to learn about "How to catch fish." He cares little for the Walton style of writing, which breathes of poesy and worms in the same paragraph, but would listen readily to this grand old angler if he were told in the brevity of a formula how to collect, preserve and use the annelids, omitting references to the nightingale's trill or the saints in Heaven. Yet, all thanks to good old Walton for his gracious advocacy of the art and to the other refined and scholarly men who have written in the Waltonian vein. In the quiet of our *sanctum sanctorum*, when the winter winds shriek and whistle outside, and the sugar-wood log burns brightly in the grate, there is nothing so enjoyable as the pages of a Prime's "I go a Fishing," or the many genial and truly idyllic sketches of a Francis, a Mather, or a Cheney.

The following endeavors to meet the case of the angler who *wants to know*, and to see at a glance the information he seeks, or where he can get it. What is here set down is the result of a long experience, and has been "boiled down" with a merciless severity, till the essence is alone presented.

THE ROD, REEL AND LINE.

The modern fly-rod, as represented by the American-made solid and split cane weapons, approaches absolute perfection as nearly as it is possible for any mundane implement to do so. The catalogues of any of the tackle makers will furnish particulars, and it is not necessary, in a little work of this kind, to do more than indicate the general characteristics of what the author, himself, prefers.

My favorite rod, therefore, is a split cane hexagonal, ten feet long, with the Orvis patent reel seat, which allows of the reel being instantly adjusted. One peculiarity of all Orvis' rods (which is the make I prefer) is that they are made with ferrules without dowels. These never loosen in the casting (because they fit true), and this cannot be said of any other rod with dowels. In English rods with dowels and the ordinary brass ferrules, which never fit accurately, it is necessary to tie the joints together with soft thread, as they would infallibly fly apart if not so tied. This results, first, from the imperfect fit of the male and female ferrule and the wedge-shaped dowel, which has the express property, owing to its form, of loosening on being shaken. Any mechanic—even knowing nothing of rods—will tell you that a tapered dowel always has a tendency to shake itself loose by vibration. Even those dowels that are not tapered are objectionable, because they impair the elasticity of the rod. As short a joint as possible should be insisted on if one would possess a useful and perfectly satisfactory rod. In these days one is so absolutely safe in the hands of a respectable tackle maker that I should only be occupying space uselessly if I dilated further on rods for fly-fishing. Let these rules guide you in your purchase : Go to a well-known, good maker, pay a fair price—cheap is generally nasty in fishing tackle—and rather get too light a rod than one too heavy, and eschew dowelled ferrules.

The name of the reels in constant use is legion. In buying, observe one thing—obtain no multiplier. A multiplier illustrates the mechanical law, every time you use it, which is stated thus : What you gain in speed you lose in force. A click or check reel of good make, with wide diameter of barrel is sufficient for anyone's requirements in trout fishing.

And now, as to the reel line. Let it ever be proportioned to the dimensions and strength of your rod. A too thin line is a greater nuisance than one too stout, and necessarily, of course, he who builds your rod will indicate the right kind of line. For my own part, I prefer one of the new "Acme" lines, patented by the Brothers Foster, of Ashbourne. Derbyshire, England, the peculiarity of which is the incorporation of a fine copper wire with the silk. In the most approved specimens of this make the wire is in the center of the line. The idea is to give a stiffness and weight to the line without increasing the size—a most important point when you are fishing with the wind against you. The great point in adjusting your fly-trout fishing tackle is to be careful that the whole tackle, from rod-butt to end of leader, tapers truly, right to the fly. I do not know of a better rule, or one more likely to facilitate the learner in the pleasant art than this, or one more likely to increase the pleasure of the "Senior Angler" by its observance. Having thus briefly touched on the subject of the rod, reel and line, I now come to refer to the leader, about which I have some more extended observations to make, as it is quite within the power of the angler to tie his own.

I need scarcely remind the reader that the gut used by the fisherman is made from the fluid silk, before it is spun, of the silk-worm. The chief part of it comes from Murcia, a Moorish town in Spain, and the longest is seldom over twenty-three inches in length. A Mr. Ramsbottom showed some of that length at the Great Fisheries Exhibition, held in London in 1883, and it was said to be the longest of the season of 82–3. Whether the larger American worms will ever produce longer gut, available and marketable, remains to be seen. Personally, I do not doubt that it will eventually be done, and I hope to have a finger in the doing. I have myself seen a single strand of gut measuring six feet in length, of good quality, of American production.

Good gut should be round and without opacity. No gut with a blemish ought to be admitted ; but as there is

so much of the best grades that are, if judged by a strict
standard, unusable, I will relax this dictum so far as to
say that the flat gut, and that which is, from some reason, brittle on being bent, need alone be absolutely con-
demned.   The spotted gut, if fairly round, may be bene-
fited by a soaking in warm water.   Thereafter, it should
be lightly stretched, and after this, and when it is quite
dry, it may be rubbed quickly and gently with chamois
leather.   This polishes the surface, and makes its appearance much more presentable than would otherwise be the
case.   If, however, the gut breaks on bending, with a
greenwood fracture—as the surgeons term it—that is,
splinters up but does not separate, reject it ruthlessly;
it is no good, and will lose you a fish when you least want
it to do so.

There are ever so many methods of making leaders,
but generally the single gut ones are tied.   Those that are
whipped together with silk are very neat when new, but
if they are used on a rocky-bottomed river, speedily become the reverse.   The whipping ravels up and becomes
insecure.   The same objection applies to those having
knots and whipped ends, and also to those joined by the
" buffer " knot, which simply consists of two " fishermen's" knots drawn tight but not close together, the inter-
vening space being whipped with fine silk.   The virtue of
the arrangement lies in the fact that no sudden strain
can come directly on the knots, but must pass through the
silk, which, of course, is not absolutely unyielding.
Hence, the leader never snaps suddenly at the junction.
So far, the idea is good but, as I have said, liable to the
objection that the knot frays.

Suppose you are determined to make your own leaders. Buy the best gut; it is cheapest. Then set to work and soak the gut. While that is soaking in cold water, (warm water loosens the fibers unduly, and should be avoided if you are not in great haste) learn to make the

Fig. 1.—SIMPLE LOOP FOR LEADER.

following knots. Figure 1 shows the ordinary loop; if you desire to make it additionally secure—supposing that to be possible—take the loop end once more through. A stout hook is necessary, as a fixture, on your work-table, and over this the loop should then be hung and pulled tight. The result should be symmetrical, and the loose end can be cut off very close. Figure 2 is a much more difficult knot to tie, but it is convenient, especially for snells, and once learned, is a very pleasing loop and ex-

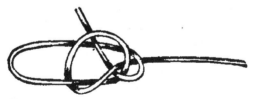

Fig. 2.—ANOTHER LOOP FOR LEADER.

tremely secure. So far as loops are concerned, I do not think it is necessary to add to these. The trout and salmon fishermen do not want any more under any circumstances, and it is folly to cram one's brains with unnecessary knowledge, which, by the bye, is an exceedingly prevalent fault, caused by the teachers of the art seeking rather to exploit themselves, than impart useful lessons.

The best junction knots in leader-making are shown at Figures 3, 4 and 5.   Take a piece of cord and practice on

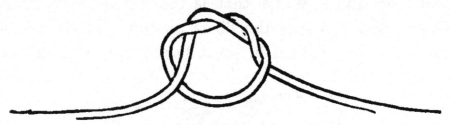

Fig. 3.—JUNCTION KNOT FOR LEADER.

it till you are perfect, then tie the gut.   Be sure to draw whatever knot you tie—tight, slowly.   The best attachment of a loop for droppers is found by placing the knot of a loop in between the component knots of either Figure 4, or Figure 5, or in the center of Figure 3.   A

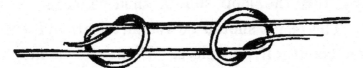

Fig. 4.—THE "FISHERMAN'S" KNOT FOR LEADER.

loop tied in, however, provides by far the most preferable method of attaching dropper flies.

If we proceed *seriatim* the fly would naturally next come up for consideration, but as I propose giving full

Fig. 5.—JUNCTION KNOTS FOR LEADER.

details of manufacture, etc., a separate chapter is necessary for its full exposition.   Lacking this at present, therefore, I propose giving details of what I consider a most important branch of the fly fisherman's education— namely, Casting.

Now, there is no better plan than for the tyro to go down to the water and patiently practice. The attitude should be easy and that which suits the angler best; it is absurd to tell a man exactly how he should stand, as if he were learning ballet-dancing, and indeed, so far as mere verbal instruction is concerned, I am conscious that I might almost as well give instructions in the "manly art

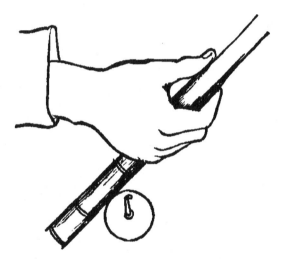

Fig. 6.—MODE OF HOLDING ROD.

of self-defence" as in the manly art of fly-casting. However, I take my chances of making myself clear and instructive by the aid of the illustrations.

The trout-rod, if single handed—and I don't favor a double handed one unless you are fishing in very wide water—should be taken in hand as shown in Figure 6, and the elbow should be kept as close to the side as possible. My father used to put me through my exercises with a small book placed between my elbow and side, and I have found this a remarkably good corrective for the disposition to swing the arm unduly. This latter does not add to the length of the cast, and certainly detracts from its neatness and precision. The fundamental idea is, "Let your rod do all the work its strength allows"—that is what it is for.

The overhand cast is that which is most generally used, and it is probably the easiest. Let out your line in

Fig. 7.—OVERHAND CAST, BACKWARD MOVEMENT.

the water, allowing the current to take it ; then recover it till the fly appears on the surface of the water. At this point, sharply throw the point of the rod back over the right shoulder, so that the line is impelled back, as shown in Figure 7. When the limit is reached, and not till then, the rod is urged forward and the cast, shown in Figure 8, is made. This movement ought to be made as the line is falling (see *b*, fig. 7), and is a matter rather for the intuitive perception of the hand than

Fig. 8.—OVERHAND CAST, FORWARD MOVEMENT.

for nice calculations on paper. If this forward throw or cast is made before the limit of the line is reached, the latter curls and snaps (see *a*, fig. 7) like a whip, and the result is the loss of your fly. Now, there isn't much in this to learn, and I purposely refrain from giving further and more minute particulars as to how this cast is made. The learner, in trying to follow the minutiæ of such detailed explanations, gets too particular and nervous—fussy, and in trying so very hard to perform what he imagines a difficult task, he throws a great deal too much conscious effort into it and fails ignominiously. Preferably, take a friend to the water-side with you who is warranted to be absolutely

Fig. 9.—THE " WIND " CAST.

ignorant of fly-casting and, necessarily, unable to criticise, and assign him the task of telling you, by a word, when the forward motion is to be made. After a short time you will come to appreciate the precise moment and can send him home. Don't be disappointed at failure. The line should fall forward, as shown in Figure 8. When you can place twenty yards out straight in front of you, as represented, consider yourself graduated as an "overhand caster."

The "wind cast" is one that is very useful when the wind is dead against one. The dotted line in Figure 9 indicates the movement of the rod in the beginning. The line must, with the full strength of the arm, be propelled up overhead and then brought down and forward, right in the teeth of the wind, till the rod's point almost touches

Fig. 10.—THE "UNDERHAND" CAST.

the water, without pause. The full strength of the rod is exerted by this cast, and the success of it is greatly assisted by the use of one of the "Acme" lines referred to a few pages back.

The "underhand cast" is made from right to left, as shown in Figure 10, or *vice versa*. This is probably the easiest of all the casts—the rod doing nearly all the work.

The "flip casts" are extremely useful when one is "negotiating" water under trees, and, indeed, the line is, in

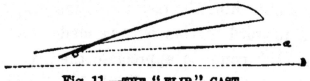

Fig. 11.—THE "FLIP" CAST.

some cases, impossible of extension in any other way. The cuts (figs. 11, 12 and 13) explain themselves. The hook is taken in the hand between thumb and forefinger (and be careful not to hook yourself!), and the rod then bowed so that on your releasing the bait it flies to the spot it is desired to reach. In Figure 11, *a* represents the path of the fly and *b* the water-line in which the angler is standing.

"Clark's spey cast" is a difficult but beautiful cast to make, and a Mr. Clark, from whom it takes its name, is

Fig. 12.—THE "FLIP" CAST.

credited with throwing fifty yards. Figure 14 shows the entire movement of the rod's point. In Figure 15 we have several movements; *a*, *b* and *c* indicate stages of the recovery from the water, during which the rod's tip describes the dotted line, Figure 14; *d* shows the result of

Fig. 13.—REVERSED "FLIP" CAST.

the downward thrash and the course in which the line should travel.

But of all casts, that explained by Figures 16, 17 and 18—namely, the "switch"—by means of which Harry

Fig. 14.—CLARK'S "SPEY" CAST.

Pritchard and his son achieve such extraordinary distance casting—stands pre-eminent. Figure 16, *a*, shows the first movement; the line is bellied, as shown from its

former outline (see dotted line) by a rapidly increasing
movement.   Now twitch the front of the rod forward by
a sharp, short action of the wrist (see *b*), causing the line
to bow in an opposite direction ; then, with a bold, ellip-

Fig. 15.—MOVEMENT IN CLARK'S "SPEY" CAST.

tical sweep (see fig. 17), from the right overhead to left,
make the downward thrash (*c*), and the line should fall
in undulating outlines, as in Figure 18.   Let the reader
take plenty of time to practice and he will not regret the
result—keeping in view the diagrams given, which are of
photographic correctness.

Having mastered the method of casting a fly with tol-
erable neatness, next turn your attention to catching the

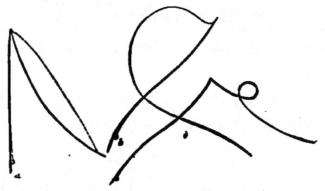

Fig. 16.—MOVEMENT IN THE "SWITCH" CAST.

fish.   The first question which presents itself is, " Shall
I fish up stream or down ?"   To this I reply, with all
the emphasis of which I am capable, "Up stream, by all
means, *whenever possible*."   There is every reason for it,
but here are a few, briefly put : (1.) Trout invariably
lie with their heads up stream—*ergo*, take their food in

that position. (2.) Trout cannot see the angler more than a few feet behind them, whilst they can and do see many yards in front. (3.) The vibration of the water, caused by the movement of the advancing angler, if

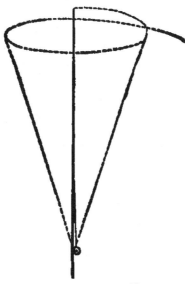

Fig. 17.—MOVEMENT IN THE "SWITCH" CAST.

wading, does not penetrate up stream as it does down stream. (4.) The water is not "roiled" or muddled for the fish by wading up stream.

These include the chief reasons for up stream fishing, and in the face of them I cannot understand there being the ghost of a shadow of reason for arguing for the down

Fig. 18.—THE "SWITCH" CAST.

stream method of fishing, except that it is easiest. I heard, only the other day, a prominent angler argue that he missed fish more frequently, because of the bellying of the line, in up stream fishing. Now, the bellying is kept taut by the stream, and the strike is thus never lost, and the fact that one strikes dead against the mouth of the rising fish instead of with a tendency to pull the fly out, as is the case when fishing down stream, renders the up stream position even more tenable than before. When it is borne in mind that the big trout of the Itchen and Test, and some other rivers of England—running up to three and four pounds—are caught by this method on flies dressed on the smallest procurable hooks (up to No. 16 Limerick), and that these wily fish, living in the most limpid of chalk streams can be caught *no other way*, the feasibility of my advice may be thought respectable. It is the fashion to deride what is termed the "old fogyism" of Europe, but I can assure the reader there is none of this commodity in its fly-fishing. The up stream, dry fly-fishing—as practised on the best rivers of the British Isles —is the evoluted result of the best inventive genius of in-telligent, observant anglers, and designed for the capture of the most artful of educated trout. The characteristics of this system of fly-fishing may be fitly detailed at this place.

As before predicated, the angler moves up, if possible, and prefers to cast to a rising fish. If he spies one ris-ing regularly, he gently walks within casting distance, the line probably trailing behind him in the water. To make the cast he urges the fly backwards and forwards twice or thrice through the air, until his quick eye sees by the flying bait that he has enough line out to allow of its falling about a yard above the rising fish. By this time the fly is dry; its swift passage through the air en-ables it to become so, and the next time it is cast right in front to the spot designated, and, when it falls, the angler watches its course without making a movement of the rod. It floats, of course, and if the fish does not take it just as soon as the radius of its circle of vision is passed, it is lifted again from the water, dried, and cast as before. If you are fishing "likely spots" instead of a rising fish, the same procedure is gone through with, and the result has ever been to me satisfactory, often beyond all expectations. Of course, on very rapid mountain streams, this method should be modified to suit circumstances, but under no existing or possible conditions is it necessary to fish down stream on an open fairly slow stream.

Some object—that motion should be given to the fly (if so, give it by all means ; fishing up stream does not prevent this !), but I would again urge that this is not necessary to be natural. Land flies, blown on the water, certainly do kick and endeavor to get ashore, but those born of water larvæ do not. Their home is on the water, where they lay their eggs and perish, and it is natural for them to flutter into air once in awhile, and then to settle down and be blown as a disruddered sailing vessel, whithersoever the wind listeth.

Supposing the fish rises to your fly—strike, not roughly but sharply, rather with a swift pulling motion than a jerk. That everlasting "turn of the wrist," which we piscatorial scribblers are so wont to recommend, is a delusion to the learner. Anything like a jerk sends the point of a fly-rod forward, unless it is immoderately stiff, and, of course, retards the hooking stroke. To make this plain, let the reader take his fly-rod and try his most artful of sharp strikes. One of the morals is, "Don't

use too whippy a rod." Always strike from the winch—
i. e., without placing the hand round the line, and for
this purpose the check should be set "stiffish."

After hooking a fish keep the point of the rod well up,
your line free to run off the winch, and yourself cool.
That is all the direction you need; the fish will teach
you the rest. Several of your largest fish, of course, will
inevitably be lost through unskilful "playing," but if I
were to write a hundred pages of directions I could not
really help the tyro. Letting the rod do its work is the
prime secret, and, of course, keeping the tip well up
allows of this. Did you ever try pulling against a strong
elastic band—I have, in training for rowing—to see
how long you could keep making efforts, and how
much your efforts amounted to in pounds, each time?
If not, take my word for it that the continued
tension is the greatest of inventions for taking the
strength out of one's muscles, and it is the same with a
fish. A good cane or greenheart rod will kill much
stronger fish, on a tight line even, than is usually be-
lieved. Check every rush of the fish, and don't be too
impatient to get him into the boat. Half the pleasures
of life lie in pursuit; conquest is "flat, stale and un-
profitable" as compared with it. Hence, I believe in
getting all the sporting power there is in a fish out of
him. I have played fish purposely till they needed no
landing net. Of course, however, the man who has the
pot to fill cannot stop to "fool around" like this.

I do not propose to give directions in reference to
salmon fishing at this time. There is an army of authorities who are better qualified to do this than I. It is

sufficient to say here that the general principles of stream "trout" fishing are applicable to lake trout fishing and the "lordly salmon." If a man is a good trout fisherman he will have no difficulty in catching salmon; but, on the other hand, there is many a good salmon fisher who makes a poor trout angler. I must not forget to say, also, that in salmon fishing the up stream, dry fly-fishing has no place, because the fly is not an imitation of any known insect. This reservation is the only one of any real importance to be made.

CHAPTER III.

TROUT FLY-MAKING.

The art of fly-dressing is a most beautiful one and more than repays him who studies it as he goes along creating things of beauty ; moreover, it grows on his inclinations, and I personally know several gentlemen, and even ladies, whose spare time is filled up most agreeably, and to their own profit, be it said, by fly-making.   Ay ! and their flies outshine, in some particulars, even the

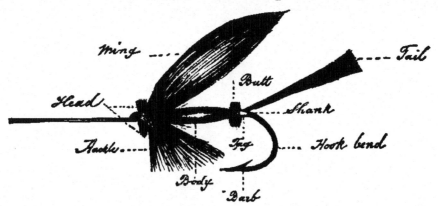

Fig. 19.—TROUT FLY—SHOWING DIFFERENT PARTS.

finished productions of professional tiers, especially in faithfulness to nature ; for, of course, one of the primal objects in fly-tying is to imitate nature closely—a fact of which the often hard-worked and badly paid professional cannot always reduce to practice, if he would.   The salmon fly is, of course, not an imitation ; rather let us call it a "poem of color," the beauty and efficiency of which depends on the variety and harmony of its component parts.

It is not remarkable that fly-making has been practiced

so long ago as two thousand years—for nothing is new but that which is forgotten—but it is strange that we find no references made to it by the ancients except Martial and Ælian. The former simply says :

> " Who hath not seen the *scarus* rise
> Decoyed and caught by fraudful flies."

But Ælian gives an account of the *hippurus* and its dressing in the following complete manner in his " *De Natura Animalium* " : " The Macedonians who toil on the banks of the Astreus, which flows midway between Berea and Thessalonica, are in the habit of catching a fish in that river by means of a particular fly called the *hippurus*. A very singular insect it is, bold and troublesome, like all its kind ; in size a hornet, marked like a wasp, buzzing like a bee. The predilection of the fish for this prey, though familiarly known to all who inhabit the district, does not induce the angler to attempt their capture by impaling the living insect. Adepts in the art had contrived a taking device (*captiosa quædam machina*) to circumvent them, for which purpose they invest the body of a hook with purple wool and having two wings of a waxy color, so as to form an exact imitation of the *hippurus*. They drop these abstruse cheats gently down stream. The scaly pursuers, who hastily rise and expect nothing but a dainty bait, are immediately fixed by the hook." According to the " *Bibliotheca Piscatoria* " this passage was first pointed out by Stephen Oliver, author of " Scenes and Recollections of Fly-Fishing," and I have transcribed it because it so clearly identifies the existence of the subject before us in the

earliest times. Moreover, it tells of the method of using
the lure—viz.: "They drop these abstruse cheats gently
down the stream," and as this is the generally accepted
mode in this country to-day, the fact is interesting.

From this period, as far as my reading serves me, a hiatus
occurs in the history of fly-making. Not until the first
book on fishing in the English language was printed, is
the subject again traceable. This fish book, the reader
needs scarcely to be told, is that of Dame Julyana
Berner's, of Sopwell Priory, St. Albans, written "to the
entent that your aege maye the more floure and the more
lenger to endure." This fair angler author advises fishing for "trowte" in "leppynge tyme" with a "dubbe,"
and at the conclusion of her treatise she gives directions
for making of twelve sorts of "dubbes for troughte and
graylynge." The details of one or two of these will suf-
fice for comparison with those I shall speak about in future pages. The doone fly: "The bodye of the doone
woll and wyngs of the pertryche." Another doone:
"The bodye of blacke woll, the wyngs of the blackest
drake and jay of the wing and under the tayle." This
work bears on the title page of the original edition,
"Emprynted at Westminstre by Wynkyn de Worde, the
yeare of Thyncarnacon of our Lord 1496."*

So much for the history of the artificial fly. To trace
it from this point to the present time would be a labor of
love of almost herculean dimensions, but quite barren

* An American edition of this charmingly quaint old treatise is published by the O. Judd Company, 751 Broadway, New York, under the
editorship of Mr. Geo. Van Siclen, an angling writer who seems to have
been imbued with a large share of the spirit of Walton in all his
utterances.

of practical results. The reader must imagine the interest it has aroused in order to fill the interregnum, and permit me to now plunge in *medias res* of the subject of its manufacture as it *now is*.

The first consideration in reference to fly-making is the selection of a hook, and it is necessary to remind the

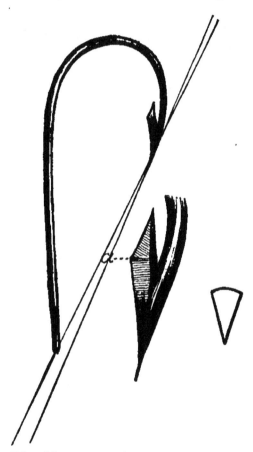

Fig. 20.—AUTHOR'S IDEAL OF HOOK.

reader of the unavoidable principles which should guide the angler in this selection. First, and chief, is strength; second, penetration; third, fouling or hooking power; fourth, holding power. Strength is a matter pertaining to the maker, and a good maker is not likely to sell a weak article. Hence, deal with a respectable firm and pay the best price—it is cheapest in the end, say I. Penetrating power depends on the point being sharp, the barb not unduly rank, and the line of impact being, as nearly as possible, coincident with the direction of force applied. The fouling or hooking power is nearly equal in all hooks with a straight vertical section—that is, not made with a "kirbed" or side twist (which injures penetration), providing all other things are equal, and the holding power depends on the nearness of the point to the opposite part of the shank, the distance between it and the first bend, and on the shape of the barb.

My own ideal of a hook is set forth in Figure 20, and I make it a present to the angling public. It has never

Fig. 21.—HOOKS OF A. D. 1496—FROM BOKE OF ST. ALBANS.

been manufactured wholesale, but the few I have made for my own use have demonstrated the unfailing accuracy of the hook in all the qualities I have named as desirable. As will be observed, the chief peculiarity of the hook lies in the form of the barb. A section of it at *A* shows it is brought to an edge razor-wise, and this is carried on down to the point. Then the slanting off of the upper part of the barb is claimed as an important improvement, allowing, as it does, of instant penetration without loss of holding power. Added to this—the line of impact is nearly coincident with the direction of force applied. (See dotted lines.) It will, I think, anyhow, be conceded that this hook is a great advance on that in use in 1496— four hundred years ago. (See Figure 21.) Another hook of high reputation on the "other side" is that brought out by Mr. Cholmondeley Pennell recently, both with tapered shank, and with an eye formed by a continuation of the shank. Figure 22 shows these hooks, though, I am sorry to say, very imperfectly. The advantages of an

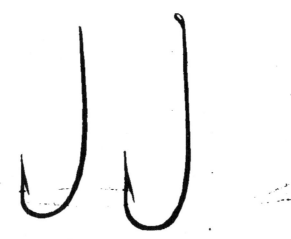

Fig. 22.—PENNELL'S EYED AND TAPERED HOOK.

eyed hook are very great—whether of the bashful or bold order.

A writer of some repute, in the "Fishing Ga-zette," June 6, 1885, thus sums up the advantages of the turn down hooks, and, though I believe my own pattern (with turn UP eye added) far superior (yet, until some firm undertakes to make it, it is practically useless), I give the opinion for what it is worth. "Hav-ing," the writer states, "made a thorough trial of flies dressed on these hooks against flies dressed on ordinary hooks with gut lappings," he thus sums up: "The result of the week's fishing, during which my worst day was four brace, and my best day nine brace [this is very good sport on English clear streams] is on every point favorable to the flies tied on to turn-down eyed hooks.

(1.) The flies never flick off.

(2.) They can be changed—attached and detached—in less than half the time.

(3.) They are stronger, because, whenever the gut gets at all frayed at the head, it can be at once shifted (re-knotted on), whereas with flies lapped on gut the weakening at the head commences very soon, and any change involves sacrificing the fly. Consequently, the fly is in many cases used long after it has become weak. But be-

Fig. 23.—THE "JAM" KNOT.

yond this there is, I think, an actual extra strength imparted by the form of knotting to the eyed hook (Mr. Pennell's 'jam' knot) as compared with the ordinary lapping.

(4.) The turn down eyed hooks appear to me to hook more fish in proportion to rises, and to lose fewer fish after being hooked. I have never met with an instance of the knot slipping."

Though it is debatable if Mr. Pennell invented the " jam " knot, or has any property in it at all, it certainly is the simplest and probably the strongest fastening for trout and grayling flies, dressed on eyed hooks, ever applied to that purpose ; while, at the same time, owing to the hook's eye having only to be large enough to pass the gut once through it, it is also the smallest and neatest.

Figure 23 shows the knot and its method of tying, in accordance with the following explanation : First—take the fly by the head with the eye turned upwards. Pass two or three inches of the end of the gut leader, previously softened by moistening, through the eye towards the point of the hook and then, letting go the fly, double back the gut and make a single slip knot (c, fig. 23) round the center link, d.

Second—draw the slip knot tight enough only to admit of its just passing freely over the hook's eye (a, fig.

Fig. 24.—" JAM " KNOT PULLED TIGHT.

23), and then run it down to and over the said eye—when, on gradually pulling the central link tight the " jam " knot is automatically formed, as shown in figure 24, which shows the fly, actual size. Finally, cut off the superfluous gut end to within from rather more than one-sixteenth to one-eighth of an inch, according to size of the hook.

For salmon flies an additionally secure knot—if such be possible—has been tested. It is shown in Figure 25, and is termed the " double-jam " knot. The method of tying it is as follows : Take the hook by the bend between the finger and thumb of the left hand, and with the eye turned downward, in the position shown in the diagram ; then—the gut being first thoroughly soaked—push the end, within a couple of inches or so, down through the eye, *b*, towards the point of the hook ; then pass it round over the shank of the hook, and again from the opposite side downwards through the eye in a direction away from the hook's point (the gut end and central link, *c*, will now be lying parallel) ; make the double slip knot, *a*, round the central link and pull the said knot itself perfectly tight ; then draw the loop of gut together with the knot, *A*, backwards (towards the tail of the fly) un-

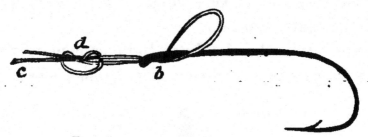

Fig. 25.—KNOT FOR SALMON FLIES.

til the knot presses tightly into and against the metal eye of the hook, *b*, where hold it firmly with the fore-finger and thumb of the left hand, while with the right hand—and "humoring" the gut in the process—the central link is drawn tight, thus taking in the slack of the knot. When finished, cut the superfluous gut end off close.

All other kind of hooks, the O'Shaughnessy and Sproat, made by Allcock, of Redditch, England, seem to me far and away the best. Allcock's Sproats in particular, are free from that vice which the other makers seem unable to get rid of—viz., breaking short off behind the barb.

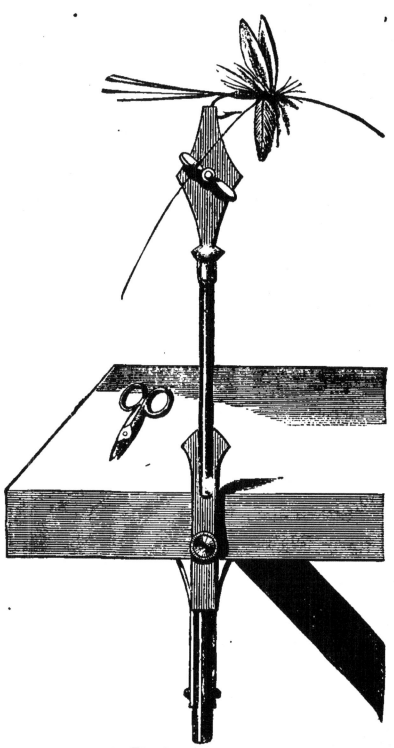

Fig. 26.—FLY VISE.

TOOLS FOR FLY-MAKING.   •

Having settled upon the hooks, the next consideration is the tools for fly-making. A great many of the old-time fly tiers use only their fingers, but the extreme delicacy of some of the smaller midges, and the intricacy of many of the chief larger flies, render the supple-

Fig. 27.—STILETTO.

mentary aid of the vise and pincers extremely convenient. Besides, I believe that it is quite impossible for an adult to learn to tie a good, strong, neat, intricate trout. and salmon fly by his fingers alone. The less handling a fly receives, the better for its appearance and workmanlike strength and integrity.

Figure 26 represents the best form of vise. I do not know if it can be bought in this country in any numbers.

Fig. 28.
SPRING PLIERS.

I can, however, put any one in the way of procuring the article if he will write to me. The engraving on page 65 fully explains its use, and needs no further comment.

Figure 27 is a stiletto exceedingly useful in arranging feathers, pricking out the wool or mohair bodies, undoing knots in the silk, etc., etc., and will, as the tyro proceeds, be looked on as a valuable assist-

ant. The same may be said also of Figure 28, representing spring pliers for holding whipping silk or tinsel, etc., at tension in the progress of making a fly, and so leaving the hands free to attend to other parts of its manufacture. They are of steel, which should be nickel-plated, or of brass—preferably the latter. The learner should have at least two pairs in his possession.

The last tool, but not least, is a pair of good, sharp-pointed embroidery or surgical scissors. They should be kept in a sheath when not being used, and never used on anything but feathers, fur or silk. Another ordinary pair will do for cutting gut.

MATERIALS FOR FLY-MAKING.

Let me, at the outset, premise that there is no hard and fast rule as to these materials, and it is in the selection of them—the perception of fitness—that the best fly-makers excel. I have seen a prominent fly-maker of this country pick a morsel out of an old sock, a couple of hairs from his own beard, and a feather from a dilapidated and decaying pigeon's wing lying by the roadside and make a fly that killed a brace of magnificent trout. But that is, of course, an extreme instance, and I only mention it to illustrate the possible variety of sources from which material may be derived. Ordinarily, the fly-maker's cabinet contains the fur and feathers of all kinds of beasts and birds. From the docile camel—the "ship of the desert"—to the mighty condor of the Andes, the fur and feather are gathered, and mean indeed is the creature that does not possess possibilities in the eyes of the enthusiastic fly-tier; again, be it said, as an ultimation, that the taste and sense of suitability for usefulness in the maker is the only guide as regards the materials of the art. Of course, generally, I may enumerate those materials that are most in use, for the benefit of the learner. After he has gone carefully a little into the processes of the beautiful art he will begin to select material for himself, and, though probably he will still continue to follow the formulas I shall give in a future chapter for the chief flies, yet he will by no means consider himself bound to them if a softer, better, or fitter material presents itself.

Briefly, then, the requisites of all fly-tiers' collections are : Silks—floss and sewing of every shade (the sewing silks are useful for whipping); the floss of the plates is simple embroidery silk ; worsteds of every shade ; cotton-batting, for making foundations of very large bodied flies ; mohair of all possible tints ; tinsel, flat, in various sizes, and oval, or of the pattern termed " flat-worm ;" chenille of various patterns and sizes ; ostrich feathers ; peacock eye feathers ; hackles—*i. e.*, feathers from the necks of "roosters" of all possible colors, especially black and white (which is a " bull," neither being colors at all). These hackles will, in many cases, require to be dyed. Next—the feathers of jungle cock, scarlet ibis, large heron, swan, wild goose, wild turkey, pin-tail duck, widgeon, teal, duck, crow, Indian crow, yellow-hammer, kingfisher, American and English jay, English, American, golden, and argus pheasant, robin, pigeon—in short, all and every bird one comes across, with perhaps the trifling exception of the carrion-eating vulture ; furs of squirrel, cat, rabbit, mole, weasel, skunk, bear, pig's wool—*i. e.*, the short hair under the bristles of a certain kind of pig ; hare's flax—the short wool under the outer coat, etc., etc.; all ought to find a place. Of course, the best of gut (not omitting the ordinary waste ends of the hank) must be included.

At the time when Blacker wrote his much overrated book on fly-making, there were no Judson's or Diamond dyes, and naturally he resorted to such as were available. Now, I cannot overestimate the value of the Diamond preparations for most of the uses required of them by the fly-maker. Be careful, however, to buy

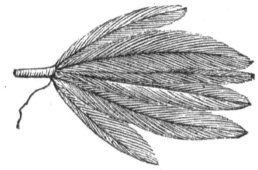

Fig. 29.—BUNCH OF FEATHERS FOR DYEING.

those sold for silk, and following the directions exactly, or the result will not be good. Figure 29 shows a bunch of hackles prepared for dyeing.

If one does not desire to go to the trouble of "bunching" the feathers, they may be dyed all together, and after being washed and pressed between a dry cloth, to remove superfluous moisture, they can be dried so as to re-establish their fibers in this way. Get a stiff paper bag and put the feathers in it loosely ; then, leaving the mouth open, stand the bag on a moderately hot stove. Of course, they will very soon get warm—and you must watch that they do not scorch—but the bag will be filled with warm air, and should now be taken and shaken with energy. This must be repeated at intervals till the feathers are dry, when they will be found of very satisfactory plumage. Some of these dyes, however, are not very satisfactory—such as the browns and their shades, and I therefore give some formulas from the last edition of "Foster's Scientific Angler," one of the most reliable and practical of modern angling books:

"In preparing a batch of feathers for staining, the uniform size required should be selected ; these should be first soaked in warm water, in which has been placed a scrap of common soap or soda; this removes the oil natural to the feathers, and enables the dye to strike evenly throughout ; when drained they are ready for the dye. In case of large feathers it may be as well, in order to strike a delicate hue, to first steep in a solution of sulphuric acid, but, generally speaking, this is uncalled for. We now append a few useful recipes for natural dyes:

FIERY BROWN.—Camwood, logwood or partridge-wood chips in equal parts, boiled in pure water.

OLIVE.—Fustic and camwood or logwood in equal parts, with a very small portion of copperas added when at the point of boiling; the last named determines the shade. The outside of large onions boiled, also, are good.

GREEN.—An infusion of fustic chips, to which must be added oil of vitriol, in a quantity sufficient to gain the shade required.

LIGHT YELLOW.—Barberry bark in solution.

DUN.—Logwood and copperas.

BROWN.—Fustic chips, two-thirds; logwood, one-third; boil in rain water.

BLACK.—One-half pound logwood chips, boil in half a pint of water ; this done, put in one ounce copperas and stir up." Gut may be stained by weak solutions of the Diamond dyes, and by any of the above.

Among the list of materials, wax and varnish must not be omitted. Cobblers' wax was for a long time used as the best; but a colorless wax made as follows is, in my opinion, the best, and takes the varnish better than any others I have used:

WHITE WAX.—Four ounces best white resin, one-half ounce fresh lard, one-quarter ounce white wax. Melt the resin first; then add the wax and then the lard; let it simmer for a quarter of an hour; then pour into a basin of cold water and pull it like taffy. The longer you pull it the whiter it becomes.

VARNISH.—Brown scale shellac dissolved in alcohol is a good varnish for flies with dark heads. Bleached shellac is better, however, producing, as it does, an almost colorless varnish. The best of all is a varnish I call the crystal varnish, made as follows: Take a quantity of the best gum copal and pick out the lightest colored and clearest nodules. Now, test them for their fitness by touching each with a drop of the oil of rosemary. If the gum becomes at once sticky where the oil touched it, it will serve your purpose. Put these pieces on one side. When you have enough, say three or four ounces, pulverize them in an iron or glass mortar, and spread the dust over a shallow dish in a thickish layer. Next, pour oil of rosemary over the layer of gum till it is just covered. Let it stand a little time, till the gum is permeated, and then stir the whole mass together. It should form a plastic, sticky paste. Now, add alcohol gradually, and it is well if you place the dish over a water bath, to aid the mixing and solution, and as soon as possible pour the whole into a bottle, adding alcohol as you think it is required to form a sufficiently thin varnish. This is a very superior varnish and will resist water much longer than shellac, though it does not dry quite so quickly.

CHAPTER IV.

LESSONS IN FLY-MAKING.

Having familiarized yourself with your tools and materials, it now becomes fit that your first fly be attempted. We will, if you please, manufacture together the "Alex-

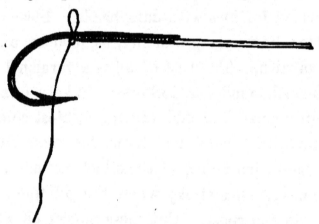

Fig. 30.—HOOK WHIPPED READY FOR DRESSING.

andra," a noted fly both here and on the "other side." It is peculiarly easy to make, considering its efficiency, and its attractive appearance when complete will commend it to the eye of the laboring tyro, hence, I select it in preference. The hooks in the illustrations are purposely shown large to aid in rendering the explanations clear.

MATERIALS REQUIRED.—Hooks, any size you prefer, but usually about number seven or eight Sproat, Pennell or O'Shaughnessy; green whipping silk, peacock herl, two whisks of any dark feather for tail, black hackle, gut.

Directions.—Take the hook between the left forefinger and thumb, place the gut underneath the hook shank, having first crushed the end of it between your teeth; begin whipping the hook and gut together, leaving about one-eighth of an inch of the shank untouched (fig. 30). Continue whipping till that part of the shank exactly opposite the point is reached, and then tie with the half

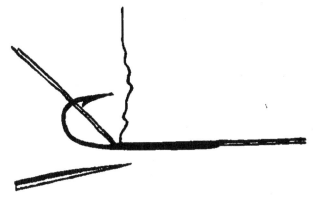

Fig.31.—SHOWING TAIL READY FOR ATTACHMENT, AND TINSEL ATTACHED.

hitch shown, drawing it tight. Of course, your silk has been previously well waxed.

Now, take two whisks or fibers of any dark feather to form the tail, and placing as shown at Figure 31, take one turn of the silk and fasten as before. Then take a piece of tinsel and attach it also by means of one turn and the half hitch knot. Then run your silk in one or two turns round the hook to end of shank, drawing it tight between the uncovered part of the shank and the gut. Now wind the tinsel evenly up the shank, holding it between the fingers or the pincers, take one turn round

it and fasten as before (fig. 32). Cut off the remaining
end of tinsel closely (but not too close), and then take
breath.

So far, so good. Your next operation is the fixing of

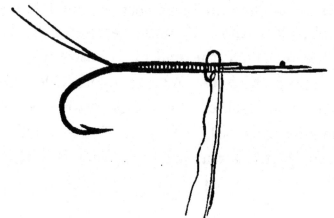

Fig. 32.—TINSEL WOUND, SHOWING METHOD OF TYING.

the hackle. Take a good hackle and draw the fibers
back between the finger and thumb until it has the
appearance shown in Figure 33. Then place the point

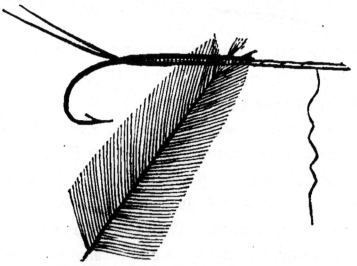

Fig. 33.—MODE OF ATTACHING HACKLE.

on the shank, as shown, and secure with a turn and
a knot: next (I am supposing you have the hook

fixed in your vise), wind the hackle round the shank
of the hook, stroking the fibres of each coil towards
the bend of the hook as it is made, to make room
for each succeeding one. Do this till the appearance
shown in Figure 34 is reached. Then, taking the hackle

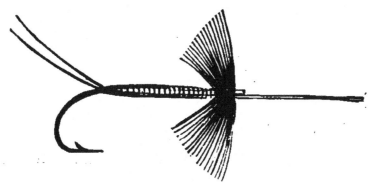

Fig. 34.—HACKLE ATTACHED AND TIED.

butt in your left hand, pass the silk once or twice
round over the hackle midrib and secure with two half
hitches. This done, cut off the loose end, and pressing
the fibers all back towards the bend, take one more turn
and half hitch to secure any of the loose fibers, that may
possibly be out of place, in their proper position. It
ought to look like Figure 34, but if it doesn't, try again.

Fig. 35.—BUNCH OF PEACOCK HERL.

It is purely your own fault that it doesn't, and there is
no difficulty in the matter that practice will not over-
come. Indeed, this is a cardinal axiom, and I must insist
on it as of ever present force in fly-making.

Now, take the curled fibers of a peacock's eye-feather

and nip off a sufficient number to form a bunch like Figure 35. Now, place them on the shank end of the hook, holding them in position between the forefinger, thumb and shank, and take a quick turn of silk over them, then a half hitch to enable you to let go of your work. See if it is straight and symmetrical; if not, gently set it right; if it is, reapply the forefinger and

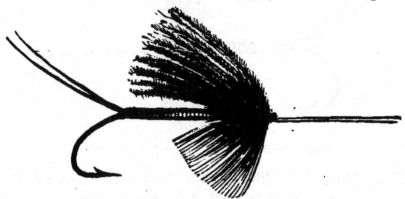

Fig. 36.—ALEXANDRA FLY.

thumb and take three or four more turns and tie with two half hitches. Touch it with varnish and your fly is finished (see fig. 36), and may thus be described:

Name.—Alexandra.

Body.—Silver tinsel.

Wings.—Peacock herl.

Hackle or Legs.—Black rooster.

Tail.—Two dark fibers.

The learner, now that he has his material and tools before him, might as well make a dozen or so of these flies, to better prepare him for the next lesson. .They will not be wasted, as they are invaluably good killers in this country, especially when the fish are at ground or midwater feeding.

Our next task is to make a "Palmer." This time we are

imitating, somewhat closely, the caterpillar of the *arctia caja* moth, and I select it for manufacture because of its educational fitness for the present purpose, irrespective of its "killing" recommendations—though these are undeniably great.

MATERIALS FOR GOLDEN PALMER.—Bright brown hackle, peacock herl, gold tinsel, orange tying silk; hook, long shanked Carlisle.

Directions.—Whip on the hook as before. Then, at the end nearest the bend, attach a strip of gold tinsel, a strip of peacock herl, and a hackle by the point; then run the silk back to the end of shank without twisting it round the shank as before, and retain it between the gut and hook, as in the case of the Alexandra. Now, twist the tinsel tightly up the shank of the hook, as in the case of the Alexandra, and fasten off. Next, take the herl and run it in a loose helix or coil up to the end; fasten off. This allows of the tinsel showing through. Now, take the hackle and wind it on the tinsel above each coil of herl but close to it, and when you get to the end of the shank take two or three turns with it close together, so as to make the hackle look "fuzzy" at the head. Tie, cut off end of silk, and varnish, and your fly is done—being thus formally described :

Name.—Golden Palmer.

Body.—Peacock herl, ribbed gold twist, bright brown hackle over all; tying silk, orange, well waxed.

MATERIALS FOR PLAIN-BODIED HACKLE.—Whisks for tail; floss silk for body; fiber of ostrich tail for head; hackle; tying silk; all these to be of colors correspond-

ing to the standard dressing of the particular kind selected for imitation.

Directions.—Whip on the hook, leaving quite a large
section unwhipped at the end of the shank ; then, by two

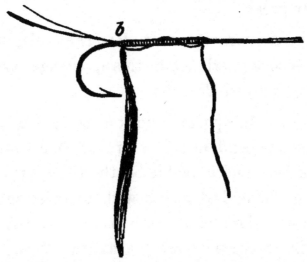

Fig. 37.—FIRST STAGE OF PLAIN-BODIED HACKLE.

turns and a half hitch, secure the floss silk (fig. 37)
and the two whisks at *b*. Having led your tying silk
up to the end of the shank and looped it between the gut

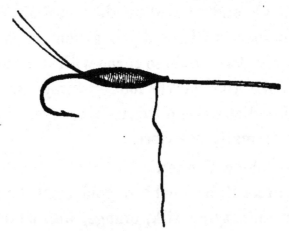

Fig. 38.—PLAIN BODY OF HACKLE.

and hook as before, take the floss silk between the finger
and thumb and wind it up evenly, as shown at Figure 38,

and secure it with a turn and a half hitch. Next, take your hackle and insert it, point before; wind it closely and tie. Cut off the loose end and varnish (see fig. 39).

Figures 40, 41 and 42 represent a Hackled Golden Palmer, made substantially on the principle of the Golden

Fig. 39.—PLAIN HACKLE FINISHED.

Palmer before described. The difference, however, is instead of the hackle running up the body it is at the head.

From the great unwinged lures of the trout I now pass to the domain of the more difficult "winged" flies. The putting on of a wing is the *pons asinorum* of the tyro, and I will let him down easily, to begin with, by explain-

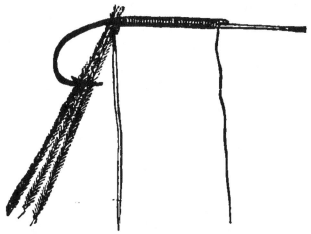

Fig. 40.—FIRST STAGE OF GOLDEN PALMER.

ing the make of the easiest winged fly I know of. This is the so-called May fly or drake (*Ephemera vulgata*), and the following is a good, useful imitation for all trout waters :

MATERIALS FOR MAY FLY.—Clean wheat straw, three strands of pheasant tippet, brown hackle for legs, and two feathers of mallard's breast for wings. Red-brown

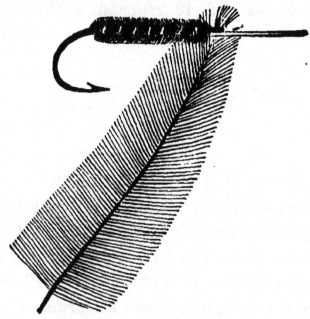

Fig. 41.—SECOND STAGE OF GOLDEN PALMER.

twist silk for ribbing. Hook, long in shank and light in build.

Directions.—First, tie on the hook to a loop of gut; fasten off, having previously whipped in the three whisks.

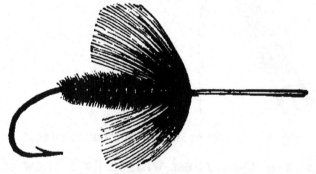

Fig. 42.—GOLDEN PALMER FINISHED.

Now, take a piece of nice, clean yellow straw and soak it a few minutes in warm water to soften it; then carefully

pare it with a sharp knife at each end till it tapers
nicely, and slip it over the loop of gut; if possible,
do all this without splitting the straw. Then, with
some red-brown silk, waxed with the colorless wax, attach it firmly by several turns opposite the point of the
hook and wind spirally up to the loop. (See fig. 43.) Se-

Fig. 43.   Fig. 44.

cure this end of the straw and the body is finished. Now
take the hackle and twist it as shown in Figure 44, and
you are ready for the wings.

The sort of feather suitable is shown in Figure 45.
Carefully proportion the sizes of the two feathers you select to the size of the body and hook, and as this fly is in-

Fig. 45.

tended to float, it is advisable to fix the feathers the con-
cave side outwards, but care must be taken that this
concavity is not too great, or a very ugly appearance is
produced. The appearance of this fly when finished is
shown at Figure 45. The particular dressing is thus
described :

GREEN DRAKE OR MAY FLY. — *Body.* — Wheaten strand ribbed with red-brown silk.

Legs.—Brown hackle.

Tail.—Three strands from pheasant's tippet feather.

Wings.—Breast feather of mallard.

Another difficult but very close imitation is made by

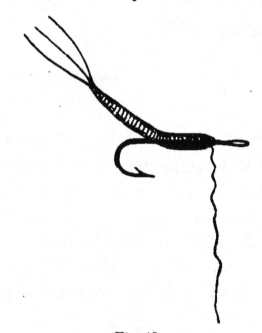

Fig. 46.

substituting a gut body for the straw, an idea of which may be gathered from Figure 46.

It is thus made : Take a length of gut, dyed yellow, and soak it till quite soft. Now, cut several pieces of stoutish gut into lengths of an inch or less, burn one end of them in a flame to imitate the real insect; these ends are placed at the end of body—the whisk or tail consists of three rabbit's whiskers. Lay all the pieces of gut together and the whisks in their place and bind round from the extremity with the strand of yellow gut. When you arrive at the center or thereabouts of the insect take your hook, previously bound on gut, and include it, carrying the coils on till the shoulder of the body is reached. Now, cut off the interior pieces of gut to a taper, and, with the waxed silk, secure the whole tightly. A hackle and wings complete the *tout ensemble*.

The making of a winged, compound-bodied, hackled and tailed fly is a sample of the higher flights of the fly

Fig. 47.—COMPOUND FLY.

tyer, and the method of accomplishing this I propose to show next. The fly I will select is an English one, containing in its make-up the separate advantages of the blue and hare's ear dun flies. It is undoubtedly a killer in this country.

MATERIALS.—Blue dun hackle, silver tinsel, hare's ear fur or mohair of a yellow and dun color mixed, yellow

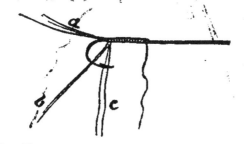

Fig. 48.—FIRST STAGE OF COMPOUND FLY

floss, red-brown hackle and dun colored feather for wings (preferably from the blue heron).

Directions.—First, take the hook and fix it in the vise; then whip on the gut as before. Next, attach the three

(*a*, fig. 48) whisks from a blue dun hackle ; then silver
tinsel, with two turns, *b* ; next, your yellow silk, *c*.
Then unravel your tying silk and take a little of the
hare's ear fur, spin it amongst the strands, as at *a*
in Figure 47.   The next process is to run it around the

Fig. 49.   Fig. 50.—FLY FINISHED.

shank and fasten off ; next, rib with the yellow silk ; then
attach your hackle and, next, the wings.   Figures 49 and
50 show the processes.

Such are the processes of making an ordinary trout fly.
A somewhat different proceeding is necessary in respect to
the manufacture of large lake trout flies, where the bodies

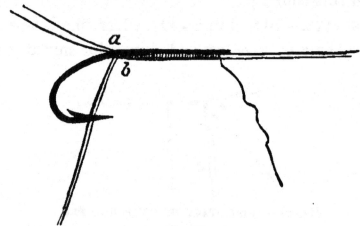

Fig. 51.

are preferred to be full and rotund.   The ordinary
"Scarlet Ibis" fly is a familiar illustration of this
(fig. 58).

THE SCARLET IBIS.—Description: Hook, No. 1 Sproat ; tag, gold cord or tinsel ; tail, fibers of ibis quill feather ; body, scarlet mohair ribbed with gold cord or tinsel ; legs or hackles, stained cardinal ; wings, two small ibis wing feathers.

Directions for Making.—Take the hook between thumb and forefinger of the left hand—or fix in the vise —and evenly bind on the gut, leaving a quarter of an inch bare at the shank end.   Next, take a length of tinsel

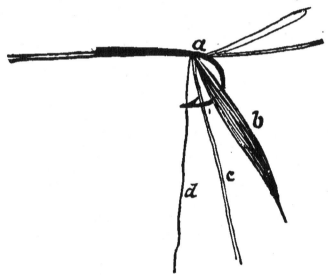

Fig. 52.—IBIS FLY, FIRST STAGE.

and placing its free end toward the shank, wrap it round, securing it with a half hitch of the whipping thread. Next take a couple or three fibers of ibis and attach them as you did the tinsel.   (See fig. 51.)   Now, take the tinsel and roll it several times at the end of the binding, which attaches the hook to the gut, to form the tag.   Tie it (see *a*, fig. 51).   Having secured it, let it hang down full, as shown ; it will be wanted presently.   Now take a portion of mohair, pulling it from the bulk and shaping it with a slight twist till it assumes the shape indicated in Figure

52, *b.*   Twist each end between the finger and thumb to a thread-like taper and attach one of them ; tie the end pointing toward end of shank by two turns and a half hitch. It will then present the appearance of Figure 52, *b.*

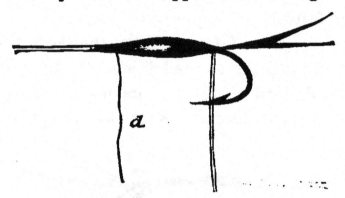

Fig. 53.—IBIS FLY, SECOND STAGE.

And here, just a word before going any further.   I want the novice to carefully go through the foregoing and to thoughtfully study Figure 52, and his work, and see that they agree perfectly up to this point.   *C* is the tinsel, *b* the mohair and *d* the tying silk.

The tying silk (*d,* fig. 52) must now be brought along the shank of the hook and looped in between the shank

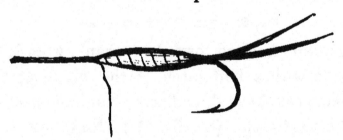

Fig. 54.—IBIS FLY, THIRD STAGE.

and gut. It is then out of the way of the next process, which consists in winding .the mohair.   Take the end and wind the strip evenly round the hook without twisting it.   It must be done so that it tapers towards the end of the shank, and for this purpose it is obvious that just sufficient mohair should have been picked out, and no more, for the purpose. If it is then properly done the appearance of the body (fig. 53) should have

Fig. 55.—IBIS FLY, FOURTH STAGE.

been attained, and it is made fast by a couple of turns of silk (at *a*) and a half hitch, the silk being again placed out of harm's reach between gut and steel, as before.

The next operation is winding the ribs. For this pur-

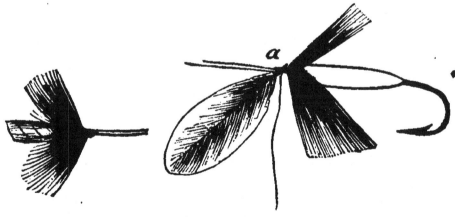

Fig. 56.
HACKLE WOUND.

Fig. 57.—IBIS FLY, SHOWING METHOD OF
TYING WINGS.

pose take the tinsel between the thumb and finger and wind it spirally up to the end of the mohair (fig. 54). Then take your pincers and secure them to it, so as to retain it in its place; release the whipping silk and take a turn and tie again, returning the silk to its place between the shank and gut.

Now select your hackle. I often use two—one superimposed on the other; they appear bushier than one only. Secure the hackle, as shown at Figure 56, with the point to end of shank, and taking your scissors snip off the point, not too close, however, or in winding you may chance to pull the hackle off, when a loss of time results, which is important if you are economical of time.

Fig. 58.—IBIS FLY FINISHED.

The hackle being secured and the tying thread placed out of the way, wind the former round the hook, stroking back the fibers of each layer with the forefinger and thumb of the left hand. This is best done by aid of the vise, and it is important, as I have before stated, that the fibers of each layer may lie straight and not be involved one with the other. (See fig. 56.)

Having wound the hackle round a sufficient number of times, the next thing is to secure it, which is done as follows (I repeat these directions to save reference back): Secure the butt end of the hackle between the fingers of the left hand or the spring pincers. Then release the tying silk and wind it rapidly and tightly round the hackle, finishing with a cloven hitch—*i. e.*, two half hitches. Next, snip off the end of your hackle and preen the fibers with the stiletto and you have the legs of the fly made as shown in Figure 56. Do not use the scissors to trim the hackle when on; this is the sign of amateurish work. Adjust the size of each part of a fly before putting it together. That is the proper way. In order

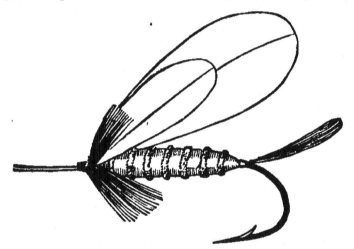

Fig. 59.—THE "QUEEN" BASS FLY.

to arrive at the right proportion, it is a good plan to buy a pattern from a first-class maker.

The next consideration is the wings. These are composed of two small feathers of equal size from the red ibis, and are first prepared by stripping off all the fluffy part nearest the end of the quill. They are then taken and neatly placed in the position shown at *a*, Figure 57, and secured by two or three turns and a half hitch of the silk. Then turn them into their proper position, holding them firmly between finger and thumb while lapping the silk round. Figure 57 roughly represents the method of thus arranging the quill end of the feather, and it is evident that if the feather be turned in this way it cannot slip or be pulled out.

The next operation is to varnish with the crystal varnish, and the Scarlet Ibis is consummated. (See fig. 58.)

Another style of fly in advance of the foregoing is shown in Figure 59. It is a "fancy" bass fly of larger

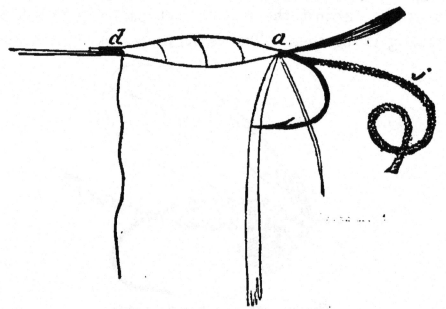

Fig. 60.—FIRST STAGE OF BASS FLY.

size than anything that has gone before. It is known to me as "The Queen," and may be thus described:

Name.—The Queen.

Hook.—'/₀ Sproat.

Body.—Yellowish green chenille over cardinal floss silk.

Tail.—Ibis, fibers of quill feather.

Tag.—Gold tinsel.

Wings.—Center feather, white goose; two outer, scarlet ibis.

Hackle.—Guinea fowl.

MATERIALS.—Chenille, of medium gauge, cardinal floss silk, ibis feathers, cardinal tying silk, guinea fowl feather, goose feather, cotton batting for filling of body, '/₀ Sproat hook, wax, varnish and gut.

Directions.—After binding the hook on, a piece of cotton batting, to form the body, is taken and moulded with the fingers round the shank of the hook. Next, attach the cardinal floss silk at *a* (fig. 60), then the ibis feathers for tail, and next, the chenille. Now, take the chenille silk and ibis right back, and attach a piece

Fig. 61.—SECOND STAGE OF BASS FLY.

of tinsel behind the others and roll it round evenly. Fasten and cut off end. Now, roll the floss silk, *a*, very evenly and tightly over the cotton and secure it at *d*. The chenille, *j*, is then wound in coils round the silk. See Figure 61. The *gallina* or guinea fowl hackle is then wound on, and this requires care. A failure or two should not daunt the learner, for in the end he will be successful.

The next operation is the placing of the wings. The large white feather is put on first and secured—be careful to crush the quill end soft before passing the whipping round it. Then the two smaller ones are put in place precisely as you did with the Scarlet Ibis fly, and Figure 59 represents the achievement.

In Figure 62 the reader has an effective kind of fly which may be thus described :

Name.—Black June.

Tag.—Gold or silver tinsel.

Body.—Peacock herl.

Hackle.—Black.

Wing.—Crow feather.

Directions.—Attach gut and tinsel as before and snip off the tinsel close.   Now, take the eye or sword feather

Fig. 62.—BLACK JUNE FLY.

of a peacock and detach three or more of the fibers; lay them close together, place the points towards the end of shank of hook, take two turns of silk and fasten; then bring the silk up the gut out of the way as before. Now, take the herl fibers and wind them together as if they were one thread on the shank of the hook, taking care not to handle the body with the warm fingers, or the little fibers will be pressed down and the appearance of the fly spoiled. Finish off as before, leaving a good space for the hackle and wings.

Now, take two hackles—you want the hackles of this

fly to be bushy—and wind them in the ordinary way, and after finishing off you are ready for the wings. These require a little preparation. Take a feather of sufficient

Fig. 63.—PIECES OF FEATHER FOR WINGS.

size, and with the left forefinger and thumb, hold about three-quarters of an inch tightly by the roots next the quill or midrib. Then, with the right forefinger and thumb, even out the ends, taking care not to break the "felting" which holds the fibers together. Now, gently but with decision, cut off a piece from a "right" feather and a piece from a "left," and fold them together, one on the other. Take these between the finger and thumb of the left hand

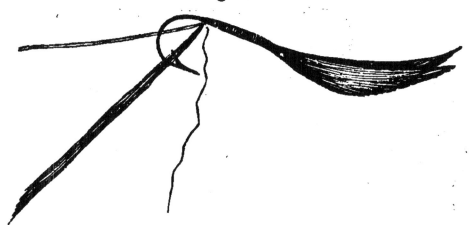

Fig. 64.—METHOD OF PLACING FEATHERS FOR TURNED HEADS.

—between the pulp of the tips, with the roots pointing to your right. Then, with the right forefinger and thumb, pinch the ends together, opening the tips of the finger and thumb to admit and retain the contracted ends.

Now, place the latter on the hook, and tightly and rapidly, taking care not to break your silk, take two or three turns round the whole and make a half hitch. Now, release your hand and look at the work done. If the wings are set right, and neatly gathered in a symmetrical taper at the base, take your scissors and cut them to a neat ending. Then dip your varnish brush and give the feather ends a slight soaking with the varnish, and then wind the silk till an even and solid head is formed. Tie, cut off the silk, varnish again, and the fly is finished.

The strongest flies are made with turned heads, and these are generally very much used in this country.

Fig. 65.—WINGS TURNED.

(See figs. 64 and 65.) In forming these flies the wing is put on first, as in Figure 64. The tinsel and body, etc., are then attached afterwards. After the hackle is tied *in situ*, the wings are then taken and firmly turned back and secured in their place (see fig. 65), and, if desired to be separated, the thread is passed once or twice between them. These flies do not, as a rule, look so neat and graceful, but their lasting power is unquestionable.

CHAPTER V.

STANDARD TROUT FLIES AND THEIR DRESSINGS.

In the preceding chapter I have given directions by which the dullest reader can make a fly of the kinds in ordinary use in this country—that is, if he will but take the trouble. In the present chapter I propose giving a list of standard flies easy to make and at the same time effective. This list is of course not intended as a representative one, but all the flies named have been proved most useful, and should be included in every well-stocked fly-book. Of course, if one cannot afford the time to learn or the leisure to tie his own flies, it is best for him to seek a reliable fly-tier who will duplicate the flies as given. To those, however, who are determined to profit by the instructions given, a few words in reference to materials generally, and the plates of material in particular, may not be deemed superfluous here. First, always endeavor to get feathers from birds of some age. Hackles—and, indeed, all feathers—are more elastic and tougher from such birds than when derived from young ones, and are, therefore, more lasting. All feathers, also, should be stored in dry, dark boxes—cigar boxes are moth repellent and of very convenient size. To absolutely prevent moth, it is only necessary to employ camphor roughly crumbled and mixed with equal quantities of napthalin crystal. The wings of birds are best, denuded of feathers, and the latter, from the right and left wings, kept separate and clearly labeled, somewhat thus: "Mallard wing—under feather—right," so that when the wings of a fly are to be selected, the right and left sides may be ready to your hand. Sometimes the right and left fiber can be picked from one feather, but that is the exception. Tinsels must not be handled, but kept in airtight boxes —a clean, dry, wide-mouthed bottle is a very good receptacle.

REMARKS ON PLATES OF ACTUAL MATERIAL.

No. 1.—*Flat silver tinsel.* This tinsel is sold in seven-yard lengths, of about five-eighth inch tinsel braid, by the gold lace makers; it is comparatively inexpensive, but if not kept from the air and damp soon tarnishes. Before using it on a fly it is not a bad plan to varnish it over with a thin coat of collodion. This preserves it somewhat from climatic influences. If tinsel tarnishes in keeping, it can be cleansed by rubbing a little alcohol over it.

No. 2.—*Flatworm tinsel.* This is far to be preferred to the wholly metallic tinsel where it can be used, but the flat is far more brilliant and scintillating in the water, and hence for immediate use far preferable. These remarks, of course, apply to the same pattern of tinsel in gold.

No. 3.—See remarks on No. 1.

Nos. 4 to 15, inclusive, are ordinary *embroidery silks,* and can be procured at any dry goods store. Pearsalls are the best and fastest colors. Of course, in using, it should be split or untwisted, one or both strands being used, according to the size of fly, etc. These silks should be kept from the light, for even the natural colored feathers of birds will fade if exposed to bright sunshine, and one cannot expect silk to stand the test better than Nature's own designed creation.

Nos. 16 to 19, inclusive, are *worsteds*, also procurable at any of the dry goods stores. In place of these, mohair is frequently used, and pig's wool—or the short hair between the bristles of a hog—and for salmon and high-priced flies, seal's fur, dyed various colors. These worsteds are split in the using and used according to size of intended flies.

Nos. 20 and 21.—*Chenilles.* These are of very useful character and ought to be used more than they are. They can be procured of any shade and thickness at the repositories of fancy silk goods.

No. 22.—*Crows' feathers.* From the wing feather choose the blackest and most evenly-tipped fibers.

No. 23.—*Grey domestic turkey.* This varies from a mottled black and white to dark brown and browny-white. It should be chosen as nearly as possible with small mottlings of black and white. Very pleasant feathers to work with.

No. 24.—*White swan, white goose, duck, hen, or pigeon feathers* from wings. Choose the thinnest at the base of fibers nearest the quill.

No. 25.—*Brown turkey tail feather.* This should be chosen whenever possible of rich dark brown and light brown, mottled regularly.

No. 26.—*Silver Black Hackle,* or white cock-a'-bond-dhu. Choose for preference very clear black tapering center, pure silver white tips.

No. 27. — *Mottled Hackle,* from Plymouth Rock chickens.

No. 28.—*Cock-a'-bonddhu Hackle.* Black center, brown tips. Acquire them whenever you get a chance They are most useful for a variety of flies.

No. 29.—*Brown Hackle.* Ditto repeated. A good hackle is short in fiber, with thin, strong mid-rib. Get your hackles as near the colors I have described as possible, but do not discard those that are near the shade but not it exactly. On the hook they look different from what they do off it.

No. 30.—*Ibis.* The feather shown is the small breast feather, and but inadequately expresses how beautiful and useful the whole feathers of the bird are. The entire skin is one blaze of scarlet, and hardly a feather is wasted in fly making. A whole skin is quite necessary to the amateur fly maker.

No. 31.—*Mallard.* This feather is from the breast of the mallard, and is given as typical of the sort of fibers required for a large variety of flies from its near relations —the wood-duck, pintail and canvasback. In all cases where this beautifully mottled feather is indicated, it is taken from the breast. The feathers from each are so similar that I do not think it necessary to repeat the others.

No. 32.—*Brown Hen.* Taken from the quill feather of a brown hen or rooster. Nearly every feather on a brown chicken is useful.

Nos. 33 and 34.—*Feather from underside of mallard wing.* These feathers provide the metallic looking dun wings of a great variety of flies and vary in shade from a white silver pearly to a dull, almost black, dun. Turn up the wing of the mallard and there they are before you.

No. 36.—*Blue Heron.* This is a very useful substitute for the dove in the Henshall, though, perhaps, Dr. Henshall would not think it an improvement. It is sometimes impossible to get the grey dove wings, and a noted Florida fisherman tells me he has substituted this feather with great advantage among the many fly rising fish abounding in the waters of that region.

No. 37.—*Ostrich herl from the plumes of the bird.* This

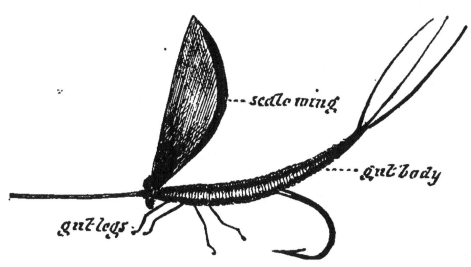

Fig. 66.—KEENE'S NEW "SCALE" WING FLY.

is exceedingly useful for the heads of flies, and makes a very attractive furnish-leader, being strong and light.

With these plates at hand, the directions themselves arranged with the most transparent simplicity, and Figure 19, page 56, showing the meaning of the terms used in reference to a fly, I leave it to the candid reader if the "force of nature can further go" in the direction of complete explanation of the subject of fly making?

ABBEY.

Body. Crimson silk ribbed, gold tinsel (Nos. 12 and 3).
Wings. Pintail duck (No. 31).
Hackle. Brown (No. 29).
Tail. Three strands tippet of golden pheasant.
Tag. Gold tinsel (No. 3).

ALDER.

Body. Peacock herl (No. 35).
Wings. Wood-duck (No. 31).
Hackle. Brown (No. 29).
Tag. Gold tinsel (No. 3).

BLACK JUNE.

Body. Black chenille (No. 21).
Wings. American crow (No. 22).
Hackle. Black.
Tag. Gold tinsel (No. 3).

BLACK GNAT.

Body. Peacock herl (No. 35).
Wings. American crow (No. 22).
Hackle. Black.

RED ANT.

Body. Scarlet silk (No. 6).
Wings. Ibis (No. 30).
Hackle. Red or scarlet, stained.
Tag. Peacock herl (No. 35).

RED SPINNER.

Body. Crimson silk ribbed, gold tinsel (No. 12).
Wings. Mallard's under feather (No. 33)
Hackle. Brown (No. 29).

Tail. Three fibers brown hackle (No. 29).

Tag. Gold tinsel (No. 3).

RED FOX.

Body. Reddish brown worsted (No. 17).

Wings. Under feather of mallard's wing (No. 33).

Hackle. Brown (No. 29).

Tail. Three strands black hackle.

Tag. Gold tinsel (No. 3).

IBIS.

Body. Scarlet silk ribbed, gold tinsel (Nos. 12 and 3).

Wings. Ibis (No. 22).

Hackle. Scarlet, stained.

Tag. Gold tinsel (No. 3).

STONE FLY.

Body. Grey silk ribbed, silver tinsel (Nos. 10 and 1).

Wings. Mallard's under wing feather (No. 34).

Hackle. Grey (No. 27).

Tail. Three fibers black hackle.

Tag. Silver tinsel (No. 1).

SILVER BLACK.

Body. Black silk ribbed, silver tinsel (Nos. 15 and 1).

Wings. Crow (No. 36).

Hackle. White with black center (No. 26).

Tag. Silver tinsel (No. 1).

SHOEMAKER.

Body. Grey and faded pink silk in alternate bands (Nos. 10 and 7).

Wings. Two pairs—inner, mallard breast wing (No. 31); outer pair, pintail.

Hackle. Brown (No. 29).

Tail. Three strands mallard (No. 31).

Tag. Gold tinsel (No. 3).

MONTREAL.

Body. Dark crimson silk ribbed, with gold tinsel (Nos. 8 and 31).

Wings. Turkey's wing feather (No. 25).

Hackle. Scarlet.

Tail. Three fibers ibis (No. 29).

Tag. Gold tinsel (No. 29).

PROFESSOR.

Body. Yellow silk ribbed, silver tinsel (Nos. 5 and 1).

Wings. Pintail duck, breast feather (No. 15).

Hackle. Brown (No. 29.)

Tail. Three fibers ibis (No. 30).

Tag. Silver tinsel (No. 3).

BROWN COFLIN.

Body. Light brown worsted (No. 17).

Wings. Under feather mallard's wing (No. 34).

Hackle. Brown (No. 29).

Tail. Three fibers black hackle.

Tag. Gold tinsel (No. 3).

BLUE BOTTLE.

Body. Blue silk ribbed, gold tinsel (Nos. 9 and 3).

Wings. American crow (No. 22).

Hackle. Black.

Tag. Gold tinsel (No. 3).

COWDUNG.

Body. Greenish brown worsted (No. 16).

Wings.   Brown hen's wing feather (No. 32).

Hackle.   Brown (No. 29).

Tag.   Gold tinsel (No. 3).

CLARET.

Body.   Claret silk ribbed, gold tinsel (Nos. 8 and 3).

Wings.   From brown hen's feather (No. 32).

Hackle.   Black.

Tag.   Gold tinsel (No. 3).

SETH GRENE.

Body.   Green silk ribbed, yellow silk twist (Nos. 11 and 5).

Wings.   Lead colored feather from under mallard's wing (No. 34).

Hackle.   Brown (No. 29).

Tail.   Three strands mallard (No. 31).

Tag.   Gold tinsel (No. 3).

SOLDIER PALMER.

Body.   Scarlet silk ribbed, gold tinsel (Nos. 6 and 3).

Hackles.   Brown ; one short up the body above tinsel, one full at head and shoulders (No. 29).

Tag.   Gold tinsel (No. 3).

WHITE MILLER.

Body.   White chenille (No. 20).

Wings.   White pigeon or goose (No. 24).

Hackle.   White.

Tag.   Orange silk (No. 4).

PALE EVENING DUN.

Body.   Yellow silk ribbed, gold tinsel (Nos. 5 and 3).

Wings.   Mallard's under wing feather (No. 33).

Hackle.   Yellow.

Tail.   Three fibers from mallard's feather (No. 31).

Tag.   Gold tinsel (No. 3).

YELLOW DRAKE.

Body.   Yellow silk ribbed, gold tinsel (Nos. 5 and 3).

Wings.   Mallard's feather, stained yellow (No. 31).

Hackle.   Yellow.

Tag.   Gold tinsel (No. 3).

YELLOW MAY.

Body.   Same as yellow drake (Nos. 5 and 3).

Wings.   White goose or pigeon, stained yellow.

Hackle.   Yellow.

Tag.   Gold tinsel (No 3).

CAMLET DUN.

Body.   Dark slate mohair ribbed, with a few coils of orange silk (Nos. 18 and 4).

Wing.   Curlew (from wing).

Hackle.   White.

Tail.   Three fibers black hackle.

Tag.   Silver tinsel (No. 1).

CALDWELL.

Body.   Claret silk ribbed, gold tinsel (Nos. 8 and 3).

Wing.   Pintail duck (No. 31).

Hackle.   Brown (No. 29).

Tail.   Three fibers wood-duck (No. 31).

Tag.   Gold tinsel (No. 3).

FERN FLY.

Body.   Straw colored silk ribbed, silver tinsel (Nos. 14 and 1).

Wings.   Pearly feather from under mallard's wing (No. 34).

Hackle.   White (No. 7).

FIRE FLY.

Body.   Red silk, plain (No. 24).

Wings.   White goose (No. 24).

Hackle.   Cock-a-bonddhu (No. 28).

Tag.   Gold tinsel (No. 3).

COACHMAN.

Body.   Peacock herl (No. 35).

Wings.   White goose (No. 24).

Hackle.   Brown (No. 29).

Tag.   Gold tinsel (No. 3).

BROWN HACKLE.

Body.   Peacock herl (No. 35).

Hackle.   Brown (No. 29).

Tag.   Gold tinsel (No. 3).

BLACK HACKLE.

Body.   Black silk (No. 15).

Hackle.   Black.

Tag.   Gold tinsel (No. 33).

GREY HACKLE.

Body.   Green silk ribbed, gold tinsel (Nos. 11 and 3).

Hackle.   Mottled hackle (No. 27).

Tag.   Gold tinsel (No. 3).

COCK-A-BONDDHU HACKLE.

Body.   Peacock herl (No. 35).

Hackle.   Cock-a-Bonddhu (No. 28).

Tag.   Gold tinsel (No. 3).

FIERY BROWN.

Body.   Brown worsted (No. 19).

Wings.   Brown hen's feather (No. 32).

Hackle.   Brown (No. 29).

Tail.   Three fibers scarlet ibis (No. 30).

GREEN DRAKE.

Body.   Straw silk ribbed, loose coils with black silk twist (Nos. 14 and 15).

Wings.   Wood-duck (No. 31).

Hackle.   Brown (No. 29).

Tail.   A few fibers of wood-duck (No. 31).

GENERAL HOOKER.

Body.   Yellow silk ribbed, six coils green silk twist (Nos. 5 and 11).

Wings.   Lead colored feather under mallard's wing (No. 32).

Hackle.   Brown (No. 29).

Tag.   Gold tinsel (No. 3).

CINNAMON.

Body.   Brown worsted (No. 19).

Wings.   Speckled brown hen (No. 32, same species of feather but speckled).

Hackle.   Brown (No. 29).

Tail.   Three strands black hackle.

Tag.   Gold tinsel (No. 3).

LAKE FLIES.

KNIGHT TEMPLAR.

Body.   Claret silk ribbed, silver tinsel—about six coils (Nos. 9 and 2).

Wings.   Equal parts white goose and black crow (Nos. 24 and 22).

Hackle. White.

Tail. Black crow and white goose, three fibers each (Nos. 24 and 22).

Tag. Silver tinsel (No. 1).

GRASSHOPPER.

Body. Brown worsted (No. 4).

Wings. Jungle cock's feather; above it one strip yellow straw color, goose, dyed, and one red ibis (No. 30), about three fibers each.

Hackle. Scarlet.

Tail. Yellow, swan and pintail duck (No. 31); three fibers of each.

Tag. Gold tinsel and one-sixteenth inch green silk (Nos. 3 and 11).

Head. Peacock herl (No. 35).

TOMAH-IO.

Body. Silver cord, flat worm pattern (No. 2).

Wings. Wood-duck (No. 31).

Hackle. Yellow and scarlet.

Tail. End of yellow hackle.

Tag. Silver tinsel (No. 1) and one-eighth inch peacock herl (No. 35).

HENSHALL.

Body. Peacock herl (No. 35).

Wings. Grey dove, small feathers or blue heron (No. 36).

Hackle. Hair from deer's tail (white).

Tail. Three strands peacock blue curled feather from sword.

Tag. Gold tinsel (No. 3).

LORD BALTIMORE.

Body. Orange silk (No. 4), ribbed black silk twist, six coils (No. 15).

Wings. Black crow (No. 22) and two jungle cock's feathers, outside.

Hackle. Black.

Tail. Crow (No. 22).

Tag. Gold tinsel (No. 3).

GREY DRAKE.

Body. White silk (No. 13) ribbed, six coils, with black (No. 15) and white silk twist (No. 47) spun together.

Wings. Mallard's feather (No. 19).

Hackle. Mottled (No. 12).

Tag. Silver (No. 13).

ORIOLE.

Body. Black silk (No. 15) ribbed, six coils ; flatworm tinsel cord (No. 2).

Wings. Swan, dyed yellow (No. 24).

Hackle. Black.

Tail. Black and white (Nos. 22 and 24).

Tag. Gold tinsel (No. 3).

NO-NAME.

Body. Yellow silk (No. 5) ribbed, silver flatworm tinsel, five coils (No. 2).

Wings. Pair small ibis feathers (No. 30), outside, white swan (No. 24).

Hackle. Brown (No. 29).

Tail. Ibis (No. 30).

Tag. Silver tinsel and red silk (Nos. 1 and 6).

CANADA.

Body. Black silk (No. 15), ribbed silver flatworm tinsel, five coils (No. 2).

Wings. Turkey wings or tail (No. 23).

Hackle. Yellow.

Tail. Small ibis feather turned flatwise (No. 30).

Tag. Silver tinsel (No. 1).

JUNGLE COCK.

Body. Scarlet silk (No. 6) ribbed, gold tinsel (No. 3).

Wings. Jungle cock's feather, single.

Hackle. White, with black center (No. 26).

Tail. Three wood-duck fibers (No. 31).

Tag. Gold tinsel (No. 3).

No. 68.

Body. Yellow silk (No. 5).

Wings. Turkey's wing feather (No. 23).

Hackle. White, with black center (No. 26).

Tail. Three fibers ibis (No. 30).

Tag. Gold tinsel (No. 3).

GRIZZLY KING.

Body. Green silk ribbed, silver tinsel (Nos. 11 and 2).

Wings. Pin tail duck (No. 31).

Hackle. Grizzled (No. 27).

Tail. Red ibis (No. 30).

Tag. Gold tinsel (No. 3).

ADDITIONAL BROOK TROUT, LAKE TROUT AND BASS FLIES IN ORDINARY USE, WITH THEIR DRESSINGS.

BROOK TROUT FLIES.

SOLDIER GNAT.

Body.   Scarlet silk.

Wings.   Brown hen.

Hackle.   Brown.

Tail.   Three fibers of a black hackle.

EMERALD GNAT.

Body.   Emerald green silk.

Wings.   Of the lead-colored under feather of the duck's wing.

Tail.   Three strands of a black hackle.

JENNY LIND.

Body.   Yellow silk, ribbed gold.

Wings.   Light blue.

Hackle.   Scarlet.

Tail.   Blue strip.

POOR MAN'S FLY.

Body.   Brown zephyr wool.

Wings.   Grey turkey.

Hackle.   White.

PHEASANT.

Body.   Yellow silk ribbed.

Wings.   Two small feathers from the English pheasant breast.

Hackle.   Brown.

QUEEN OF THE WATER.

Body. Yellow silk with brown hackle carried up palmer-wise.

Wings. Mallard breast feather.

Hackle. Brown.

OLIVE GNAT.

Body. Olive green silk.

Wings. Same as Emerald gnat.

Hackle. Brown.

Tail. Three fibers from brown hackle.

ETHEL MAY.

Body. Green silk, gold tinsel.

Wings. Black and white feather of guinea fowl.

Hackle. Brown.

Tail. Three fibers of a black hackle.

CHANTRY.

Body. Peacock herl.

Wings. Brown turkey.

Hackle. Brown.

ORANGE BLACK.

Body. Orange, ribbed gold.

Wings. Black.

Tag. Gold.

Tail. Three fibers of golden pheasant tippet.

STEVENS.

Body. Dark green silk.

Wings. Same feather as Emerald gnat.

Hackle. Small feather of ruffled grouse.

KING OF THE WATER.

Body. Cardinal silk.

Wings. Mallard breast.
Hackle. Brown.

MARCH BROWN.

Body. Dark brown wool, ribbed gold tinsel.
Wings. Dark brown turkey.
Hackle. Brown.

WIDOW.

Body. Blue silk, ribbed silver tinsel.
Wings. Same as Emerald gnat.
Hackle. Black center, white tips.
Tail. Three strands of a black hackle.

DARK STONE.

Body. Dark brown wool.
Wings. Dark brown mallard.
Hackle. Brown.
Tail. Two fibers of a brown hackle.

BLUE PROFESSOR.

Body. Dark blue, ribbed gold.
Wings. Mallard breast feather.
Hackle. Brown.
Tail. Scarlet ibis.

BLACK GNAT.

Body. Black silk.
Wings. Black bird or crow.
Tag. One turn of ostrich herl.
Hackle. Black.

LAKE TROUT FLIES.

THE BEE.

Body. Ostrich herl ribbed with light yellow chenille.

Wings. The brownest part of the tail feather of the wild turkey.

Hackle. Coch-y-bonddhu.

BLUE BOTTLE.

Body. Blue silk, ribbed gold tinsel.

Wings. Crow.

Hackle. Black.

ROYAL COACHMAN.

Body. In four sections: first, scarlet silk; second, ostrich herl, two turns; third, scarlet silk; fourth, ostrich herl, three turns.

Wings. White goose.

Hackle. Brown.

Tag. Gold.

Tail. Barred wood-duck.

FERGUSON.

Body. Yellow silk, ribbed gold.

Wings. Brown turkey surmounted by two strips of yellow-dyed goose.

Hackle. Green and yellow mixed.

Tail. Scarlet ibis.

BASS FLIES.

WHITE AND JUNGLE COCK.

Body. Colored silk, ribbed gold tinsel.

Wings. Inner bar white goose, outer bar chenille cock.

Hackle. Scarlet.

Tag. Green silk, gold tinsel.

Tail. White, black and red strips.

BLUE JAY.

Body. Silver tinsel.

Wings. Blue, white and black feathers from the jay's wing.

Hackle. Black.

Tag. Scarlet chenille.

Tail. Barred wood-duck.

BLACK AND GOLD.

Body. Yellow silk, ribbed gold tinsel.

Wings. Crow surmounted by two strips of the yellow swan or goose.

Hackle. Black.

Tag. Gold.

Tail. Black and yellow strips.

CALIFORNIAN.

Body. Yellow silk ribbed with gold tinsel.

Wings. Mallard breast feather stained yellow.

Hackle. Yellow.

Head. Black ostrich.

Tail. Yellow goose and two strips of peacock herl.

Tag. Gold.

PREMIER.

Body. Scarlet silk, ribbed gold.

Wings. White goose or dove, with two outer wings of red ibis.

Hackle. Scarlet.

Tag. Gold.

Tail. Red ibis.

THE DAVIS.

Body. Yellow silk, ribbed silver.

Wings. Brown turkey.

Hackle.   Green mixed with yellow.

Tag.   Silver.

Tail.   A strip each of red and yellow goose.

ALEXANDER.

Body.   Silver tinsel.

Wings.   The curled part of the sword-feather of the peacock.

Hackle.   White.

Tag.   Red silk and gold tinsel.

Tail.   Same as wings.

FITZ MAURICE.

Body.   Half scarlet and half black chenille.

Wings.   Mallard breast.

Hackle.   Yellow.

Tag.   Gold.

Tail.   The curled fibers of peacock sword-feather.

TRIUMPH.

Body.   First section, green silk ribbed with gold; second section, brownish-yellow chenille.

Wings.   Crow.

Hackle.   Black.

Tail.   Three strips of green parrot.

Tag.   Gold.

POLKA.

Body.   Cardinal silk ribbed with gold.

Wings.   Two feathers from the guinea fowl.

Hackle.   Scarlet.

Tag.   Gold.

Tail.   White and brown feather.

LA BELLE.

Body.   Light blue silk ribbed with silver.
Wings.   White goose.
Hackle.   Blue.
Tag.   Red silk and gold tinsel.
Tail.   A fiber each of white and red swan.

THE INTERCHANGEABLE ARTIFICIAL FLY.

An invention of my own which I believe will eventually prove to be a great boon to the artificial fly fisherman is a device I have named as above. It consists, as may be seen in Figure 67, of an artificial fly made in two detachable parts. The body and tail of the fly are

Fig. 67.—THE INTERCHANGEABLE FLY.

tied on the hook in the ordinary way, except that down the center of the body is placed a tube of quill, the entrance to which is shown at *A*. The head, wings and legs or hackle of the fly are tied on the pin *B* as shown. In order to join the two parts together, it is only necessary to enter *B* in the tube *A*, and press the head of the pin : a perfect fly is thus formed, which in no wise differs in appearance from any other ; indeed, it is rare that the junction between the parts of the fly is observed by the uninformed.

The advantage of this arrangement is obvious, especially in regard to bass fishing, where a fancy fly is always used. It is well known that bass are exceedingly capricious, and whilst they will not take some colors at all, they will bite freely at others. Very often it happens that the angler has only one or two patterns with him, or perhaps at the most a dozen ; none in the case we are now supposing will attract the fish. If he have, however, one dozen different-colored bodies of the interchangeable fly, and one dozen heads, wings and legs made up of different colors, he can produce 144 different changes from the one dozen hooks on his line. A gross of these flies allows of nearly 21,000 different changes. The principle can be adapted to the larger trout flies used for lake trout, and also to salmon flies.

The details of manufacture are simple enough. In building the body of the fly a strip of quill of any thin kind is soaked in hot water, then rolled around an ordinary pin, and placed alongside of the shank of the hook. The silk or other material is then wound around firmly and over it, and fastened off securely. Two coats of varnish should be applied to the whipping, and allowed to harden thoroughly. By the time the varnish has become hard, the quill tube will also have dried in position ; and my experience is that it will remain firm, notwithstanding hard usage, until the entire fly becomes a wreck. The pin is now withdrawn and placed next in the vice, and the wings and hackle tied on it securely.

This is all there is to the "Interchangeable" fly, and I think every fly-fisherman will look upon the device as at least a most useful one, especially in the woods, where economy of space and adaptability should be encouraged to the uttermost.

FLOATING FLIES.

During the last year or two a good deal of attention has been attracted to the subject of floating flies; *i. e.*, flies that are intended to float down on the surface of the water in the manner of a natural insect. This style of fishing is termed fishing with the dry fly, and the floating quality is generally maintained by the angler waving the rod twice or thrice before delivering the fly on the water, and by this procedure freeing the fly entirely from moisture, so that it floats buoyantly on the stream.

The floating fly fishing mode comes to us from the chalk streams of Southern England, of which Kingsley and others have written so charmingly. There the Itchen and Test softly flow at a slow, easy rate of progress between the lush-grown banks of water meadows, and the flies which rise to the surface are nearly all of the gauzy winged species comprised by the *Neuroptera* and the *Ephemeridæ*. The water being extremely clear at all times, and not very deep, the fish are wary above all their compeers. To fish for them successfully, one must stalk them from behind, up stream. Fishing down stream in the American style would be utterly useless. A rising fish is carefully watched for, and he is approached from behind with most cautious and stealthy movement, and the tiny imitation of the fly on the water at that time is finally thrown above where the fish lies, and thus allowed to float over it. It is needless to say that if any of the flies in the foregoing part of this book were used for this purpose, they would not fulfill the floating part of the arrangement. The wing in all ordinary American flies is too small, and the hook too heavy, to allow of the fly floating, and, indeed, there is no general necessity for floating flies as yet in the rivers of this country. There are some streams, it is true, in Pennsylvania and York State, where the education of the fish demands some sort of different treatment to that extended to the wild trout of the wilderness. On these streams the tiny midges and gnats, which have

Fig. 68.—UP-WINGED QUILL-GNAT.

been found so successful in the South of England, have done great execution. Figure 68 shows the ordinary up-winged quill-gnat. The wings are placed in the position shown, and consist of small segments of a starling quill-feather, or of a part of the under feather of the duck's wing.

In order to increase the floating power of these small flies, it is now customary to double the amount of the wing, placing on two pairs instead of one pair, as shown in Figure 69. Figure 70 shows the same fly after it has been cast two or three times, and when the wings have become separated in the natural course of events. Nothing can exceed the life-like appearance of these tiny flies as they float on the surface of the water attached to a gossamer gut snell and leader. These wings are chiefly adapted to the so-called quill-gnats. The quill in the make of this fly is derived from the peacock eye feather, as will be described further on, and it forms a very dura-

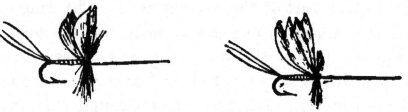

Fig. 69.—DOUBLE-WINGED FLY.　Fig. 70.—DOUBLE-WINGED FLY
AFTER USING.

ble and life-like body, at the same time being exceedingly light.

Of course this double winging is not applicable to the larger members of the May-fly family. In their case, as shown in Figure 71, a cork body is mounted on the shank of the hook, and a pair of mallard breast-feather

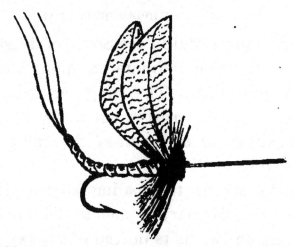

Fig. 71.—CONCAVE-WINGED MAY-FLY WITH CORK BODY.

wings (No. 31), cut to shape and stained the right shade, are attached. The legs are formed of a properly-colored hackle, and the head of the fly consists of a strip of ostrich herl. In order to render the cork plastic, it is

customary to soak it in hot water, and in order to shape
the body and render it sufficiently rigid, a piece of tin
or aluminum wire should be placed in the center. A
selected colored, stout whipping silk forms the ribs of
the fly, and attaches it, as shown, to the shank of the
hook.

In Figure 72 we have another form of floating fly, the
wings of which consist of four hackle feathers tied on

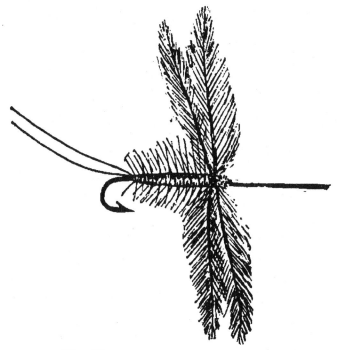

Fig. 72.—FORM OF FLOATING FLY.

outstretched, as shown. The body may be made of the
dried husks of Indian corn, and should be hackled without its entire length, as indicated in the diagram. This
fly is supposed to represent a spent May-fly lying inert
and dying on the surface of the water. It is occasionally very deadly, even on American streams, as I have
had occasion to find out.

FLOATING BAITS OTHER THAN FLIES.

An imitation of members of the beetle family is often very effective on the much-fished streams, and, indeed, on streams of any kind. Figure 73 gives an idea of the class of bait I mean. It represents more or less correctly the ordinary June-bug of this country, and "chafer" of England, and in my hands it has been very deadly. I usually dress it in this way: Attach the hook to the gut strongly, then tie on at the bend of the hook, which will be the tail end of the hook, four or five strands of peacock herl. Next take a broad strip of any cinnamon-colored feather, such as the brown feather from the peacock's wing, and, pinching the fibers

Fig. 73.—IMITATION JUNE-BUG.

of one end closely together, attach that end also to the hook by the side of the peacock. Now take the peacock and wind it up the body about one-third the entire length. Insert here two mid ribs of two brown hackles. Continue with the herl one-third further, and then bring out the two free ends of the mid ribs to form another pair of legs. Continue with the herl, and before fastening it off at the head, place in two more midribs to form the front legs of the bug. At the same time, place in two fibers of horse-hair to form the feelers. Now take the herl up to the neck of the fly and tie it in securely. Form a head of ostrich herl; tie off neatly; go back and take the cinnamon-colored feather; stretch it up to the neck of the fly over the back and tie securely. Varnish, and the bug is made.

It will be seen in the foregoing that I have omitted to mention the cork necessary for those bugs whose large size compels them to be used as floaters. The only difference in their construction is that a thin strip of cork is tied tightly on the shank of the hook immediately after it is attached to the gut of the hook. Other imitations are made in a somewhat similar manner. That of the black cricket is best effected by framing the body from black worsted, using crow's feather to cover the worsted in. Two small equal feathers form the wings, and legs may be pieces of waxed silk passed through the thorax of the bait by means of a needle.

The ingenuity of the angler will suggest to him the suitable materials if he has followed me thus far in fly-making, and I need not go further into particulars under this head.

QUILL-GNATS.

The small floating flies referred to on the preceding page are usually made with quill bodies. I casually mentioned that this quill was derived from the peacock "eye" feather, but I think a little additional explanation as to the manufacture of these very useful and beautiful creations may not be out of place.

In selecting the quill, or rather the fiber from which the quill is derived, an experienced fly-tier takes a bunch of peacock eye feathers and turns them over, holding them obliquely, so that the light falls upon the reverse side in a slanting direction. He then picks out the lightest-colored feathers, and from these strips the fibers which form the chief part of the eye pattern. Taking one of these strips between the finger and thumb, he deftly with his nail strips the fibers. Figure 74 indicates the appearance of the strand with the part of the fibers stripped off. It will be seen that one-half of the strip is of a dark color, and the other light. This forms the material of the quill-bodied gnat. Quills are also occasionally stripped from other feathers besides the peacock when a single colored body, such as that of the black gnat, is required, but ninety-nine one-hundreds of all quill-gnats have the bodies made of this material.

It is seldom that the peacock fiber can be got either completely black or white on either side. In order to whiten it, it may be so immersed in ozone bleach or dioxyde of hydrogen. This has the effect of rendering the white part completely colorless, and has no material

Fig. 74.—STRIP OF PEACOCK FIBER.

effect on the darker band. These strands may be dyed any color required to imitate a natural insect by means of the Diamond Dyes. The great secret in dyeing, however, is to use a small amount of dye ; see that all feathers or quills have been soaked in a hot solution of alum to remove grease, and plenty of fresh cold water should be employed in rinsing.

The advantage of this quilled strip is that its banded appearance closely imitates the actual appearance of the small flies so frequently found hovering over running water. When detached bodies are required, the inner core of the body is formed of hog's bristle softened in warm water and bent to shape as required.

Of course all these small flies are exceedingly difficult to manage at first attempt, so that the fly-tier who would succeed with this must bear in mind that his only royal road is practice! practice! practice!

THE "DIAPHINE," OR SCALE-WINGED FLY.

Some years back, in 1884 I think, a writer in the English "Fishing Gazette," styling himself "Bittern," wrote thus: "What is really required is a substance which combines the lightness and buoyancy of the feather in the air as well as in the water, with the toughness and power of the quill to retain its shape, together with the pliability and transparency and texture of the gold-beater's skin, and the property of being easily stained or dyed; and this material, so far as I know, has yet to be discovered."

This was, I know, a considerable time after the late Mr. MacNee had put on the market his PIKE-SCALE winged fly. I mention this because it has rather important bearing on what follows. "Bittern" wrote in full knowledge of the inefficiency of the pike scale as a wing, it being hard and quill-like under all circumstances.

For many days I searched for the material required, and ransacked from stores of feathers and other resources, lest haply I might light upon something fulfilling the requirements pointed out. At that time I was staying with my father, who was Queen Victoria's fisherman in the Windsor Great Park, and he and I carefully canvassed the whole subject.

One morning, whilst I was still busy with this problem, my father came in with two large Rudd (a fish somewhat like a "Shiner")—the largest, I think, I ever saw. They had been taken from a carp pond near the house, and were in the very height of condition. He prepared them for the royal household, and I gathered up the scales that fell from them, intending to make some flies for my own use with the Rudd scales instead of those of a pike.

On cutting one of these through with the shears, I accidentally separated the fine membrane, which lines the underside of all scales, from the hard structure of the outer or upper side. I immediately saw that I had discovered the material I was in quest of, and set to work at once and dissected a score or two of these scales, detaching the membrane, which was easily done after cutting around the edge of the scale with a pen-knife. The properties of this membrane were remarkable. I found it perfectly transparent, and so tough that no effort of mine with teeth or nails was sufficient to tear it, although its thickness could not have been as great as that of the paper upon which this is printed. Whilst it was wet, it was perfectly pliable; but although it could be bent in any direction at the slightest touch of the fingers, it instantly resumed its shape on being released. When dry it was somewhat stiff, but not nearly so much as the pike scale, and when wet it was incomparably more ductile.

On experimenting further I found that it took a lukewarm dye or stain admirably; moreover, its specific gravity was only slightly greater than water itself.

As I was leaving England shortly after this, I did not make many flies myself of this material, but, before departing for this country, I communicated with Messrs. Foster Bros., of Ashbourne, Derbyshire, and imparted the method of preparing this material to them. Coming hither, I also showed the Mills Bros., of Warren Street, New York, how the material was detached from the scale, using, I recollect, a shad scale for the purpose.

I thus go into particulars because it is asserted that this invention of mine invades that of Mr. MacNee, and I wish once for all to make it plain that it does not. Mr. MacNee's fly-wing was made from the soft belly scales of large pike. It was claimed that the calcareous matter of these scales was dissolved out of them by some process, but it is certain that any dissolving process sufficiently potent to make a solution of the horny part of the scale would infallibly dissolve the fine membrane beneath it. I have several of the MacNee flies before me now, and, though they are extremely well tied and elegant in appearance, it is obvious that the wings are too quill-like to be perfectly satisfactory.

I have called the membrane for the sake of distinction "Diaphine," from its diaphanous texture. It is to be found on the under side of the scales of all the smooth scale-fishes, from the herring to the tarpon. Personally I employ the scales of the shad, the buffalo fish, and the tarpon.

So far as very small flies were concerned, this membrane answered admirably. I had absolutely no fault to find with it. In a word, it exactly was described by "Bittern" in the passage before quoted. But when larger flies in this country were winged with it, it was found that, as the fly was propelled through the air, the material was not stiff enough to prevent its rustling to such an extent as to render the noise unpleasant, and to impede the swiftness of the cast. Although these are not insuperable objections to its use, yet I foresaw that

it would never be popular with the dilettante angler, and
therefore set about endeavoring to find a remedy.   This
remedy I have found, so that the wing no longer flutters
as before, and at the same time, though it is more rigid,
it is not too rigid to suit the fish.   To make the dif-

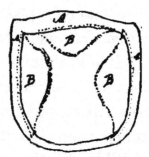

Fig. 75.—OUTLINE OF A FISH-SCALE.

ference plain, let the reader look at Figure 75, which is
an outline of the lining membrane of a scale of a buffalo
fish.   Formerly I used to cut it from the scale in the
shape indicated by the inner black line, but I now
detach it, preserving a horny surrounding, shown at *A,
A, A*.   In cutting the wing, I do it as indicated by the

Fig. 76.—MAY FLY, SCALE-WINGED.

dotted lines, so as to preserve a proportion of the horny
border of the membrane.   *B, B, B*, indicate the ordinary shape of a wing.   This horny border, mounted as
shown in Figures 76, 77, 78 and 79, retains the wing
rigid as it passes through the air, and the noise and

retardation complained of formerly, therefore, do not
exist. In these diagrams the wing is shown in its
native transparency, but of course it is stained according to the pattern of the fly for which it is destined.

From the fact that it is only susceptible of being
stained one color, it is obvious that it is not suitable for

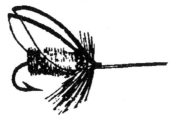

Fig. 77.—COACHMAN, SCALE-WINGED FLY.

the imitation of those flies wherein several colors are
visible on the wings : hence it does not *absolutely* fill the
bill as an exact imitation. Figures 76, 77, 78, 79 and
80 indicate some of the uses to which it can be put with
advantage, and an observant angler will look around
and find a very large proportion of the fishermen's flies
which it will exactly counterfeit. In some cases it may
be veined with a fine pen dipped in either of the Dia-

Fig. 78.—STONE FLY, SCALE-WINGED.

mond Dyes, but I cannot say that the veining is entirely
a satisfactory result when done.

Figure 76 is a May Fly with gut body. In place of
hackle it has legs composed of fibers of turkey feather
tied in as shown. Figure 77 is the ordinary Coachman.
Figure 78 shows the Stone Fly. Although the wing

here is transparent, it would be, when made, stained of a dark brown color by means of a strong infusion of coffee.

Fig. 79.—BLACK ANT, SCALE-WINGED.

Figure 79 is the Black Ant, made with black silk body and black hackle at head; head of ostrich herl and transparent "diaphine" wings. Figure 80 is one of the

Fig. 80.—SCALE-WINGED MIDGE FLY.

small Quill Gnats with transparent wings. Figure 65, page 99, is a fly I make for trolling, and, though not very beautiful, it is useful.

THE "INDESTRUCTIBLE" FLY.

The Indestructible Fly cannot be better introduced to the reader than by a letter I received from Dr. George Trowbridge in 1887, referring to one I had made him for Florida fishing. He writes from Sarasota, Fla.: "The fly has made the following score: February 22, four sea-trout, one skip-jack. February 23, six sea-trout, one channel bass of seventeen pounds; this is probably the largest channel bass ever taken with the fly by any one. February 23, eleven sea-trout. February 25, nine sea-trout, one cavaille, one grouper, one rock-fish. While lifting a small sea-trout into my boat, not using the landing net, the old and frayed leader broke, so I cannot return the fly for your inspection. The greatest damage was done to the hackle, which was almost entirely destroyed." Thirty-five fish on one fly!

Knowing as I did the extraordinary tenacity of the "Diaphine" wing, I procured some tarpon scales, some of which measured nearly three inches in diameter, and from these I detached a membrane which was of a thickness and area suitable for the complete making of large flies. In the specimen before us (see Figure 81) the hook is tied on to a loop of twisted gut. The tail con-

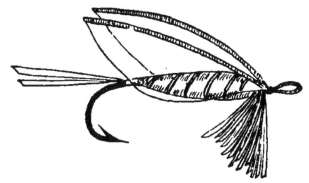

Fig. 81.—THE "INDESTRUCTIBLE" FLY.

sists of two slips of the tarpon membrane dyed scarlet. The body is built up of colored silk; over this a strip of the membrane is wound, so as to completely incase the silk. Over this, in turn, are six ribs of flat worm tinsel. This tinsel hides the junctions of the coils of membrane, and therefore the body has a most polished and elegant appearance. The hackle or legs consists of slips of the membrane also dyed scarlet. The wings are, of course, cut from the membrane of a tarpon scale of fit shape and size. The whole is put together very strongly, and it is almost impossible for the ordinary bass or lake trout to tear it to pieces. In the case of the fly referred to by Dr. Trowbridge, I had used a yellow rooster hackle, and this showed signs of wear the first. In my own experience, I use one of these indestructibles until I am absolutely tired of seeing it around. It is immensely useful for bass and general trolling.

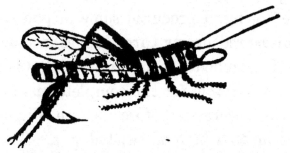

Fig. 82.—GRASSHOPPER, SCALE-WINGED.

Grasshoppers may be made in a similar way (see Figure 82), substituting strips of tarpon membrane for the hackle midribs, as shown in use for legs.

WATERPROOF WINGED FLIES.

One of the difficulties with all feather winged-flies, if they be large, is the fact that they become very soon demoralized in appearance and water-logged. For example, the Montreal, either as a bass or trout fly, has a wing contrived from the tail feather of the turkey. This looks and is admirable for the first two or three casts, but after this the fibers separate, the water penetrates and soaks the feather, and it loses all its antecedent beauty. The difficulty was to find a means of waterproofing and adding to the coherence of the fibers of the feather without rendering it too stiff or unmanageable. I tried collodion and shellac varnish, and various oil varnishes and other applications, until it occurred to me to use a solution of the pure rubber (caoutchouc) in chloroform. The under side of the feather is painted with this and allowed to dry in the sun and wind. The result is an immense improvement, and I recommend its adoption on all bass and light trout flies, where the wing is derived from the side of a quill feather.

I have found it extremely useful in securing a cohesion of wings that are married, to use a technical expres-

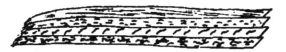

Fig. 83.—" MARRIED " STRIPS FOR WINGS.

sion (that is, composed of strips from the feathers of different birds welded into one wing). (See Figure 83.) I also have found that it is enduringly lasting when the wing is rolled. (See Figure 84.) This rolled wing, by the bye, may be used on smaller flies even of the midge size with great advantage, especially if painted with the solution of rubber.

Fig. 84.—ROLLED WING.

I would warn all amateur fly-tiers against the use of oils of any and all kinds in the preparation of feathers with the intent to waterproof them. The oil is so exceedingly apt to penetrate to the whippings of the fly and loosen the work.

"EXACT IMITATION" ARTIFICIAL FLIES.

I have always been greatly in favor of the exact imitation theory and practice of fly-making. I cannot see the least justification for an indifferent imitation artificial fly, when there is the possibility of making the simili-

tude an exact one. That being the case, I have persistently for many years advocated an exact reproduction in
imitation of the flies and other insects used in fishing,
and have persistently ransacked the resources of natural
history and nature generally for suitable material. The
thousands of experiments I have carried out would be
impossible of enumeration at this time, even if such
were profitable.

The materials and manufacture of the fly I am about
to describe are the latest developments at which I have
arrived.

I take it for granted, of course, that the angler desires

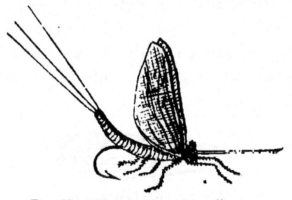

Fig. 85.—"EXACT IMITATION" FLY.

his artificial fly to be as nearly as possible, in form, color
and texture, a duplicate of the actual prototype. Figure
85 shows my conception of what this should be, assum-
ing that the original is one of the *ephemeridæ*. The
body of the fly is formed of gut, quill, or silk, or other
material most resembling the fly to be imitated, according
to the judgment of the maker, and wound around a sufficient number of hog's bristles. The legs are composed
of the midribs of hackles carefully selected for their
flexibility and tenuity. In Figure 86 is shown the

method of winding this body, and in Figure 87 the
reader perceives when to affix the legs.   Of course if
the finer and more spring-like *hackle* is preferred, there
is really no reason why it should not be used.   In swiftly

Fig. 86.—WINDING BODY OF "EXACT IMITATION" FLY.

running water I incline to the use of the hackle rather
than the midrib, for the reason that the water sets
against the fine fibers and bends them out of position ;
they in turn springing back, and thus creating a life-like
movement, which would naturally in the troubled water
become a simulacrum of life.   In quiet streams I use the
fly shown (Figure 85), without adding any outside movement to it.   As it floats down it appears to be a dead fly
blown on the surface of the water, and as such I am
able to state is uniformly successful.   The *wing* of this

Fig. 87.—HOW TO FIX LEGS OF "EXACT IMITATION."

fly is without question the most complete imitation of
the natural wing yet in existence.   Figure 88 shows my
method of preparing it ; and in its explanation, *A* is a
fine gauze stretched over the vacant place in a frame as

shown, *B* is the midrib of a hackle which is threaded through in and out the meshes of the gauze. This forms the backbone, as it were, of the wing, and renders it stiff without being unnatural. With a fine camel's-hair pencil the natural tracery on the wing of the fly to be imitated is drawn in suitable colors (the gauze of course being of the same hue as the ground color of the wing of the insect). When the wing is thus satisfactorily colored and the midrib placed *in situ*, a coating of a water-

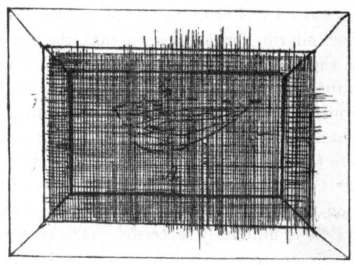

Fig. 88.—METHOD OF PREPARING WINGS OF "EXACT IMITATION" FLY.

proofing preparation is carefully laid on the gauze. This fills the interstices of the material after it is dry. Sometimes another and yet another coating is necessary, but ordinarily one is sufficient. Sometimes it is necessary to attach fibers of feather or silk to indicate the ribbing of the wing, but ordinarily this is not necessary. After the waterproofing solution is dry, the wing can then be cut out and presents the appearance shown in Figure 85. If the right gauze be used and the right solution, the result is at once the most exquisitely natural and at the same time most durable imitation.

Objection has been urged against detached bodies,
such as the foregoing, on account of their inflexibility
owing to the stiff bristles forming the core. To obviate
this I am occasionally in the habit of fabricating an extremely flexible body, as follows. It is thus made (see
Figure 89) : *A* is an ordinary fine sewing needle tightly
fixed in the vice, as shown. *B* is a thin slip of dentist's
sheet rubber. *C* are three fibers to form the tail. *D* is

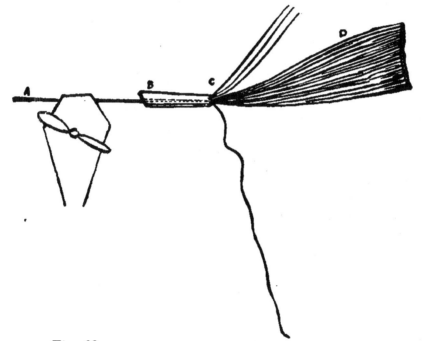

Fig. 89.—HOW TO MAKE FLEXIBLE BODY OF FLY.

a strip of some close felted feather; and all these are tied
in together as shown. The next operation is to turn *D*
back towards *A* ; cover the rubber *B* completely, and
wind silk thread, which should be of the proper color for
ribbing, around the tiny slip, until the body presents the
appearance shown in Figure 90.

It should be finished off on the needle as indicated
(Figure 90) and the needle can then be withdrawn. The
body will be found perfectly secure, owing to the elasti-

city of the rubber, and can now be placed on the hook in a manner similar to that pursued in reference to Figure 85. When finished this fly shows the perfection of pliability and durability. Another device for securing

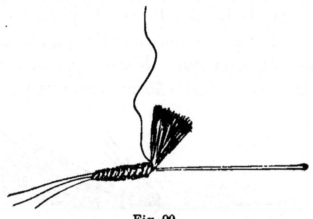

Fig. 90.

flexibility of the body when detached is shown in Figure 91. In this case, the hinder part of the body is made separate with a loop, as shown at *A*. This loop is of gut, and the body itself is a core of this material instead of bristle. It is placed as shown in Figure 91 on the hook, and if the hinge be made rather tight in its

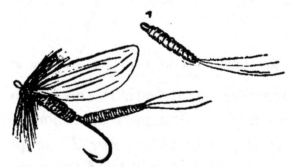

Fig. 91.—JOINTED BODY FLY.

bearing, the body can be adjusted before casting in any position desired. I am of the opinion that this is a decided improvement, although it is not absolutely preferable to that shown in Figure 90.

I am perfectly aware that in some of the foregoing descriptions much is novel, and indeed new to the ordinary reader—new even to the expert, in some instances. In concluding this section, however, I will say, that I shall be very pleased to explain by personal letter anything that seems ambiguous, and it will afford me pleasure to assist the tyro with samples of materials, etc., and in any other way that seems convenient, if he will apply to me, either through the publisher or directly to the address given in the front part of the book.

FLIES WHICH CAN BE DRESSED WITH THE SCALE MEMBRANE OR "DIAPHINE" WING.

Coachman,	Hawthorne,	Yellow May,
Lead-winged Coachman,	Widow,	Black June,
Royal Coachman,	Stebbins,	Jenny Lind,
Red-tipped Coachman,	Orange Black,	Morrison,
Cowdung,	Gen. Hooker,	Katydid,
Fern Fly,	Deer Fly,	Hoskins,
Red Ant,	Red Fox,	Iron Dun,
Black Ant,	Soldier,	Brown Coflin,
Seth Green,	Grey Coflin,	Emerald Gnat,
Teal,	Fire Fly,	Black Gnat,
Red Spinner,	Beaver Kill,	Soldier Gnat.

The above list is part of the ordinary standard patterns. All the smaller gnats and duns, and indeed most of the smaller flies, can be very successfully imitated in the above material.

THE ABSOLUTELY SIMPLEST AND QUICKEST WAY TO MAKE A TROUT OR BASS FLY IN THE WOODS.

This is the solution of a problem that occupied my attention quite a long time this last winter, though it was presented to me by a small boy only. Said he, while watching me putting a tiny quill-gnat together, "That seems about the hardest kind of a 'chore;' can't you show me the easiest way to make a fly?" It was for some days a poser, but I think I have got the solution, and if it benefits only one angler who finds himself in some out-of-the-way locality where abides no tackle-maker, I shall have my reward in his gratitude. And so, to plunge *in medias res* of the explanation, here is how to do it.

Suppose you have a snelled hook in your possession; you can find a piece of thread; you also want a hackle from the neck of a rooster, and a couple of feathers from *opposite* sides of some bird, if possible; and you also want something for the body—wool from your knit socks will do, or a tuft, dirty as it is, from the back of a sheep isn't so very objectionable. I have caught bass with just such a body.

Now, to get to work. Take the thread—if it is waxed it is, of course, all the better—and tie it at *A* (Figure 92). Run it up to *B*. Then take your hackle, *with the under side up*, and tie it as shown at *C*, with two half hitches. Next take your two feathers. They may be from a hen or pigeon, and should be made to match each other. Crush the ends flat between your teeth, so that they will lie close when tied. Place them exactly as shown at *B*, and tie securely. Now bring forward

the thread *D* along the gut out of the place.   It will
not be again used for a little while.   The next thing to
do is to take the hackle between the finger and thumb

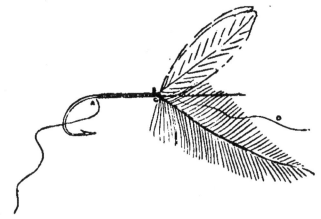

Fig. 92.—FIRST STAGE.

and wind it sidewise around the hook shank at *B* and
C (Figure 92), until the appearance shown (Figure 93)
at *A* is produced.   Now bring up your thread (see *A*,
Figure 92) to *B* (Figure 93), and tie the hackle, bringing
the end of it alongside the shank, as shown at *C*.   It
now becomes necessary to make a body.   Take a piece
of worsted or yarn of the color you want—or, indeed,

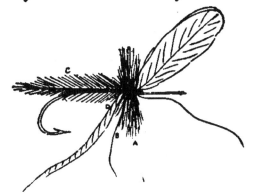

Fig. 93.—SECOND STAGE.

any color or material that is handiest, providing it is
not too extraordinary—and attach one end at *D* (Figure 93).   Next pass your thread to the bend of the hook

out of the way, and proceed to wind on the body over
the hackle and along, till it presents the appearance of
Figure 94.   Tie it with the thread, and that securely,
with three or four hitches, and cut both the wool re-

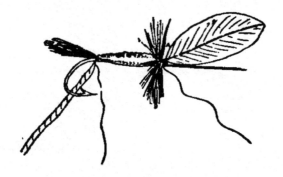

Fig. 94.—THIRD STAGE.

maining and the thread off close.   The next operation
is the final one.   Take the wings shown at *A* (Figure
94), turn them back toward the bend of the hook, tie
them there as shown at Figure 95 at *A*, cut off the
thread, and your fly represents a compact creation simi-

Fig. 95.

lar to Figure 95, and capable of doing good work on **any**
lake or stream where the necessary fly-taking fish abound.
Now, if anybody can tell of a simpler winged, tailed and
hackled fly, I beg to call him forward.

FLY BOOKS.

Mention of a receptacle in which flies should be kept, so as to at once be at hand and perfectly safe, should be made at this time. All the foregoing flies, and indeed all flies of all descriptions, can be tied on eyed hooks,

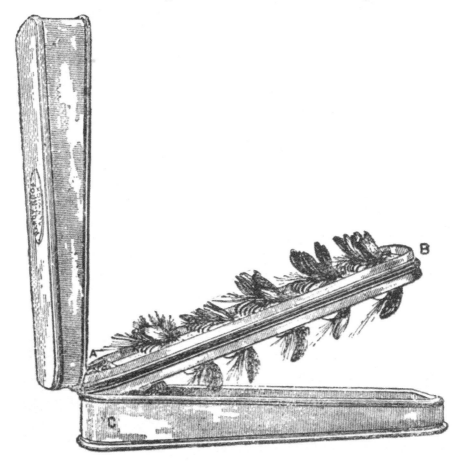

Fig. 96.

similar to that shown in Figure 22, page 61 ; and when this is the case, something different to the ordinary fly book is required to keep them separate and in good condition. Figure 96 shows the most convenient receptacle I have yet seen for the eyed fly. *C* indicates a top and bottom lid. *A* and *B* show a tongue or frame, along which ridges of cork are firmly secured. Into these ridges the flies may be hooked and kept securely, and at the same time immediately at hand. This case can be made, of course, in various sizes, and is easily stowed away in the pockets, being neither cumbersome nor of awkward shape.

If the flies, however, are tied on the ordinary gut snell, I know of no better arrangement than that to be found in the shape of the Bray fly book (see Figure 97). The flies are hooked over a convenient bar, and a gut

Fig. 97.

snell is brought straight back and lodged between the coils of a coiled wire spring. These coils are brought so closely together as to constitute a spring of gentle tension ; hence the fly can be instantly placed in the book securely, and is instantly detached when required. I repeat that I know of nothing in the shape of fly books equalling or excelling the device shown in Figure 97.

SALMON FLY MAKING.

Very few words introductory are necessary in reference to this branch of fly-making. It is undoubtedly the fine art of the fine art of fly-making, and a good fly-tier is a man whose tastes and faculties generally approach very nearly to those of a true artist. The fly-tier is at once the artisan and artist.

The art of salmon fly-tying is not, as might be supposed, so intensely difficult, after the difficulties of ordinary fly-tying are once surmounted. The tyro who has carefully learned the separate stages of the trout fly, although he may fail twice and even thrice in his endeavors to make a salmon fly symmetrically and well, will ultimately accomplish his task ; he needs only perseverance. The man who can make a quill-gnat has no excuse at all for being unable to make a salmon fly.

MATERIALS NECESSARY FOR SALMON FLIES.

Of course the materials of a salmon fly are more numerous and varied than is the case with the trout fly, however elaborate it may be. In the Jock Scott salmon fly there are nearly forty pieces of material in all, and in one of Mr. Kelson's latest patterns, which he calls the " Chatterer," there are some three hundred to four hundred different feathers in the body alone. I do not mention these instances to scare the learner, for they are exceptional, and the majority of salmon flies are much simpler. It is well for the learner to collect plenty of the following materials, so that he may not be at a loss if a difficult pattern is desired to be made.

Feathers of summer duck, pintail, golden pheasant, and swan, mallard, bustard, blue macaw ; hackles of all colors, guinea fowl, golden pheasant ; blue feathers of the chatterer, Indian crow, red-bird, toucan, turkey, peacock wing, argus pheasant, different colored ostrich feathers, jungle fowl ; in fact, almost every feather of supremely good color is useful. Added to these, all kinds of tinsels are indispensable; all kinds of the finest embroidery and floss silks. Seals' fur in all colors, mohair in all colors, wools, and chenilles are also requisite.

THE HOOK.

There are several kinds of hooks used in salmon fly-making, and the selection of one in particular is a matter entirely for individual preference. For my own part, the Dublin Limerick pattern is good enough, but

Fig. 98.

in order to make the most graceful and secure fly, I think the newly invented salmon hook is perfection. The shank, instead of tapering as is the case with most other hooks, has a small knob formed (see Figure 98), which allows of the feathers being tied very tightly, and

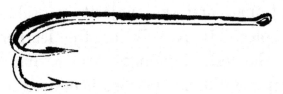

Fig. 99.

of an exceedingly neat head being made. Some anglers prefer a double hook. Figure 99 shows a double-eyed hook which can be tied very securely, as shown on page 64. This also enables one to make an exceedingly elegant and neat fly.

Having selected the hook we will now proceed to make a salmon fly, commencing with the easiest pattern of which I know. This pattern is an elaborate arrangement of hackles, and differs only from the ordinary

Fig. 100.—THE GLOW-WORM.

hackle fly in that it possesses three instead of one set of hackles. The name of the fly in question is the "Glow-worm" (Figure 100), and it is found to be particularly captivating under many conditions. Its dressing is as follows :

Body. Copper-colored chenille.

Hackles. Three in number as illustrated, increasing in size, are coch-y-bonddhu.

Tail. Ibis.

Tag. Silver twist and yellow seal's fur well picked out, making quite a tuft.

Now, any one who can make a hackle can make one of these glow-worms. The hook is placed in the vice, and the silver thread wound on for the tag. Next, a small bunch of seal's fur is rolled with the forefinger in the palm of the left hand : unless this is done the seal's fur will be found to be quite unmanageable. It is then taken and rolled around the waxed silk thread, and this in turn is taken once or twice around the hook, in such a manner as to place the seal's fur in shape like a small tuft.   A rather wide strip of red Ibis is now tied in for tail ; next comes the smallest of the three hackles ; then

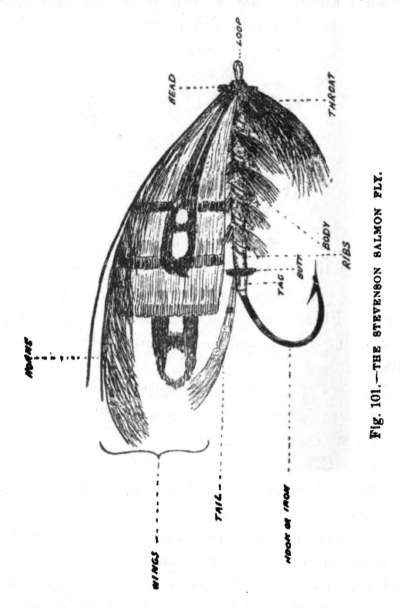

Fig. 101.—THE STEVENSON SALMON FLY.

the chenille ; then the next largest hackle ; chenille again, and finally the largest hackle of the three ; finish off, and varnish, and the fly is made.

Of course this pattern can be varied almost infinitely,

and experiments tried according to the fancy of the fly-tier. Flies made after this principle are also exceedingly good for bass and lake trout, and I wonder they have never been more extensively tried in this country.

Before I proceed to give instructions for the manufacture of the winged salmon flies, it would be well if the student cast a glance at Figure 101 wherein I have indicated the separate parts of the salmon fly and their names. When he has done this, we can proceed to build the fly (a "Stevenson") that he sees before him in Figure 101. The dressing of this fly may be thus described, and all the feathers indicated should be on the table ready for use.

Tag. Silver twist and light blue silk.

Tail. A topping and strands of the tippet.

Butt. Black herl.

Body. Two forms of orange silk, orange seal's fur having an orange hackle down it.

Ribs. Silver tinsel (flat) preceded by silver lace.

Throat. A light blue hackle.

Wings. Four double tippets as shown, back to back, enveloping a couple of extended jungle cock feathers and a topping above.

Sides. Jungle.

Horns. Blue macaw.

Head. Black Berlin wool.

HOW TO MAKE THE "STEVENSON."

Place the hook firmly in the jaws of the vice, and tie on your loop of gut securely. Take a piece of silver thread or twist and roll it around for the tag. Next take a piece of light blue silk. Roll it around carefully, and tie off, cutting off the waste ends, of course. Now take a topping of suitable size, and two or three strands of golden pheasant tippet, tie in as shown, and secure with the customary half-hitch knot. Now take a strip of black herl, tie in one end, and roll it around about twice, finishing off as before. We now come to the body. Tie in orange silk, some flat silver tinsel and silver lace, and the orange hackle at a point just beyond the ostrich herl. Tie these in very securely; wind the silk on about one-eighth of the length of the shank. Then take some orange seal's fur and roll it between the palms until it felts somewhat together. Spin it on the waxed thread and roll it in taper form, growing larger up the shank to the shoulder of the fly. Now take the silver tinsel and roll that in four coils up the body; follow this by the silver lace; then take the orange hackle and wind that in a position just preceding and next to the silver lace. Tie at the shoulder, and you have the body finished.

Now take an ordinary blue hackle and tie it in the ordinary way, as for a trout fly, at the shoulder. We are now ready for the wings. These consist of four double tippets, back to back. Between these are placed a pair of jungle cock's feathers, and outside of the tippets another pair of jungle cock's feathers are tied in; over these is placed a good long topping, and above this come the horns. The head consists of black Berlin wool, and is rolled around as shown. Two half-hitches and a little varnish complete the fly, which after all is not so very difficult a one to make.

I think if the careful reader will study the foregoing illustrations and instructions, he will find no difficulty in tying any of the salmon flies in ordinary use. Of course, there are others exceedingly more difficult, but they are all based on the same principle. The following are the dressings of a few which have been found to be especially killing.

SILVER DOCTOR.

Tag. Silver twist and dark yellow silk.

Tail. A topping. (Lately the inventor adds Kingfisher).

Butt. Dark scarlet wool.

Body. Silver tinsel (flat).

Ribs. Silver tinsel (oval).

Throat. A blue hackle and Gallina.

Wings. Connected strands of tippet, summer duck, pintail, golden pheasant tail, swan dyed light yellow and light blue, mallard, and bustard, with a topping.

Horns. Blue macaw.

Head. Dark scarlet wool.

THE BLACK PRINCE.

Tag. Silver twist and very dark yellow silk.

Tail. A topping.

Butt. Black herl.

Body. Three equal divisions of silver tinsel (flat), butted with two black feathers from the nape of the Indian crow at the termination of each section, and peacock herl.

Wings. Five or six golden toppings.

Horns. Blue macaw.

Head. Black herl.

THE GOLDEN BUTTERFLY.

Tag. Silver twist and light blue silk.

Tail. A topping.

Butt. Black herl.

Body. Light yellow silk. The body is divided into five sections, butted with a tippet feather above and below on either side, slightly increasing in size, and black herl as illustrated.

Ribs. Fine silver twist.

Wings. Six toppings (more for larger hooks, less for smaller).

Horns. Blue macaw.

Head. Black herl.

THE MAY QUEEN.

Tag. Silver twist and very dark yellow silk.

Tail. A topping and Indian crow.

Butt. Black herl.

Body. Two turns green macaw silk, and the rest silver tinsel (flat).

Ribs. Silver tinsel (oval).

Hackle. Blue macaw, as illustrated.

Throat. Tinted yellow macaw.

Wings. Two tinted yellow macaw feathers, taken from the red-bird, back to back as shown, and a topping.

Cheeks. Enameled thrush (large).

Horns. Blue macaw.

Head. Black herl.

BLUEBELL.

Tag. Silver twist and dark orange silk.

Tail. A topping.

Butt. Black herl.

Body. Blue silk.

Ribs. Silver tinsel and silver lace.

Hackle.   As illustrated, powdered blue macaw.

Throat.   Yellow macaw.

Wings.   Red macaw (in strands).   Two toppings above.

Sides.   Jungle fowl.

Horns.   Blue macaw.

Head.   Black herl.

GITANA.

Tag.   Silver twist and blue silk.

Tail.   A topping and chatterer.

Butt.   Black herl.

Body.   The first short half silver tinsel (flat), as shown, ribbed with tinsel (oval).   Over this there are two Indian crows, back to back, top and bottom, butted with black herl.   The rest, black silk ribbed with gold tinsel (oval) and silver tinsel (flat), and having a natural black hackle along it from the first turns.

Throat.   Green macaw (the feather is taken from under the wing or tail of the bird).

Wings.   Two blue macaw feathers (taken from the top of the wing), jungle on either side, extending beyond the tag, with three tippets overlapping on either side, the first reaching to the butt, and two golden toppings above.

Horns.   Red macaw (double).

Cheeks.   Blue chatterer.

Head.   Black herl.

THE GREEN PARROT.

Tag.   Silver twist and dark orange floss.

Tail.   A topping, teal, and red and green parrot.

Butt.   Black ostrich.

Body.   Pea-green floss.

Ribbed.   Oval tinsel.

Hackle.   Grass-green, from first turn of tinsel.

Wings.   Fibers of tippet; broadish strip of peacock wing; bustard, pheasant tail, teal, red-green and yellow swan, with a topping over all.

Cheeks.   Jungle (two spots).

Horns.   Blue macaw.

Head.   Black wool.

THE SAILOR.

Tag.   Silver twist.

Tail.   A topping.

Body.   Equal sections of bright yellow and light blue fur.

Ribbed.   Oval silver tinsel.

Hackle.   Greenish blue over the light blue fur.

Wings.   Double strip of finely marked teal, on either side; topping over.

Cheeks.   Chatterer.

Head.   Black wool.

THE BARON.

Tag.   Silver twist and dark red claret silk.

Tail.   A topping.

Butt.   Black herl.

Body.   In two sections. The first half with silver tinsels (flat), ribbed with silver tinsel (oval), butted again with herl and Indian crow, as shown. The rest with black silk and silver twist, having a dark red claret hackle along it, and jay at the throat.

Wings.   Tippet strands and swan dyed yellow, summer duck, blue and red macaw, golden pheasant tail, peacock wing, two strips of mallard above, and a topping.

Sides. Jungle fowl.

Cheeks. Chatterer.

Horns. Blue macaw.

Head. Black herl.

THE CHAMPION.

Tag. Silver twist and light yellow silk.

Tail. A topping, unbarred summer duck, and swan dyed light crimson and very light blue.

Butt. Black herl.

Body. Light blue silk, followed by equal quantities of dark yellow, crimson, very dark crimson, very dark blue, and black seal's fur.

Ribs. Silver lace and silver tinsel (oval silver tinsel for small patterns).

Hackle. Natural black, as shown.

Throat. Jay (dyed gallina for large patterns).

Wings. Two summer duck feathers (back to back), partially veiled at bottom with married strips of silver pheasant and golden pheasant tail (twice), and blue macaw and swan dyed light crimson (once), alternating with broader strips of teal, as illustrated; strips of unbarred summer duck, swan dyed crimson and dark yellow, peacock wing, golden pheasant tail, and also two of mallard above, with a topping.

Horns. Blue macaw.

Cheeks. Chatterer.

Head. Black herl.

BRITANNIA.

Tag. Gold twist (double quantity).

Tail.　A topping.
Butt.　Black herl.
Body.　Red orange.
Ribs.　Gold tinsel.
Hackle.　Red orange down the body.
Wings.　Shovel duck and a topping.
Sides.　Jungle fowl.
Cheeks.　Chatterer.
Horns.　Blue macaw.
Head.　Dark blue hackle.

THE GORDON.

Tag.　Silver thread and orange (medium) floss.
Tail.　A topping and Indian crow.
Butt.　Black ostrich.
Body.　Four turns orange (medium) floss, the remainder claret-color floss, medium shade.
Ribbed.　Silver tinsel and silver twist.
Hackle.　Claret, to match body, from orange floss.
Throat.　Greenish-blue hackle.
Wings.　Two tippets, back to back, extending to butt, with a rump feather (red) projecting about one-half inch; bustard, pheasant's tail, peacock wing, dark brown mallard, blue-red and yellow swan, and a considerable quantity of bronze herl; topping over all.
Sides.　Jungle (two spots).
Horns.　Blue macaw.
Head.　Black wool.

BLACK DOG.

Tag.　Silver twist and yellow floss silk.
Tail.　A crest and a few fibers of scarlet ibis.
Butt.　Black ostrich.

Body. Black floss silk, ribbed with gold and silver oval tinsel, orange floss run in between the two tinsels; black heron hackle at shoulder.

Wings. Bronze peacock herl, silver-grey turkey, bustard, pintail, teal, wood duck, mallard, swan feathers dyed red, yellow, and blue, jungle cock at each side, blue macaw crest over wing.

Head. Black wool.

If the fly is to be dressed larger than above, a black cock's hackle is run down over the body. The Black Dog is one of the very best Tay flies, both for spring and autumn. It has been used on the Tay over sixty years, but with a plain silver-grey wing instead of a mixed wing.

INFALLIBLE.

Tag. Silver twist and light blue silk.

Tail. A topping.

Butt. Black herl.

Body. Three or four turns of claret silk, followed by very dark yellow silk, having a claret hackle running along it.

Ribs. Broad silver tinsel (flat).

Throat. Jay.

Wings. Double tippets, back to back, surmounted with golden pheasant tail, peacock wing, bustard, mallard, red and blue macaw, and a topping.

Sides. A narrow strip of summer duck.

Horns. Blue macaw.

Head. Black herl.

BLACK RANGER.

Tag. Silver twist and dark yellow silk.

Tail.   A topping and ibis.

Butt.   Black herl.

Body.   Black floss silk, having a natural black hackle run down it, as shown.

Ribs.   Silver tinsel (oval).

Throat.   Light blue hackle (dyed).

Wings.   Four golden pheasant tippets, back to back, enveloping two projecting jungle fowl feathers, and a topping above.

Cheeks.   Blue chatterer.

Horns.   Blue macaw.

Head.   Black herl.

PHŒBUS.

Tag.   Silver twist and blue silk.

Tail.   Two toppings and chatterer.

Butt.   Black herl.

Body.   In four equal sections of gold tinsel (flat); butted as before, having toucan and Indian crow, as illustrated.

Wings.   Two green macaw feathers, back to back.

Sides.   Summer duck, as shown.

Cheeks.   Chatterer, two toppings over.

Horns.   Blue macaw.

Head.   Black herl.

The foregoing are flies to be made according to the orthodox methods. I have purposely omitted the hook size, as that should be regulated by the fishing to be done. Sometimes flies dressed on the largest sizes, equalling, say, a No. $\frac{3}{0}$ sprout, and at other times as small as No. 4, are best. As a rule, however, salmon flies vary from Nos. $\frac{2}{0}$ to 3 in size of iron. I have tied them on a No. 12 hock for brook trout, but I need scarcely enlarge on the difficulty of securely fixing some score or more pieces of material on so tiny a piece of steel.

There *are* variations in the method of salmon fly-making, of course. For example, the "Spey" flies have the hackles very long, soft, and wound the reverse way all through. There is also a killing device in the artificial prawn tied with feathers, silk, etc., and I have samples of a "spinning" or trolling fly which revolves by means of two fan-like flanges; it is said to be deadly, but hard to manage. The foregoing are suitable for American and Canadian waters, however, and are all of most attractive appearance and standard character, being "killers" wherever fairly tried.

THE END.

CPSIA information can be obtained
at www.ICGtesting.com
Printed in the USA
LVOW04s1913290817
546826LV00009B/450/P